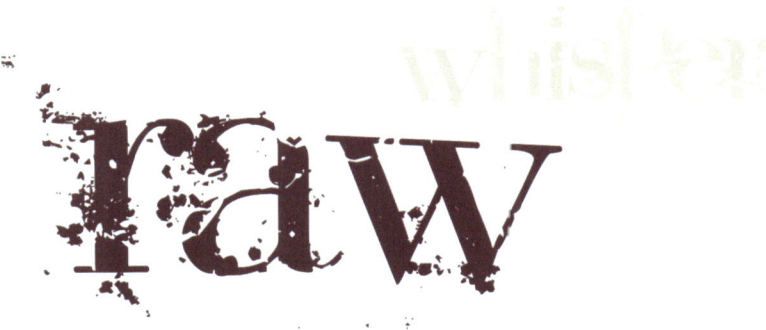

raw

Okanagan Erotic Art Show 2009

Compiled by Julia Trops
Foreward by Alissa Woodside

June 1 - 30 2009

A Woodside Design Gallery
1561 Pandosy Street
Kelowna BC V1Y-1P5
PH: (250) 862-3817
info@awoodsidedesign.com

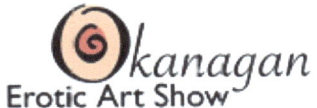

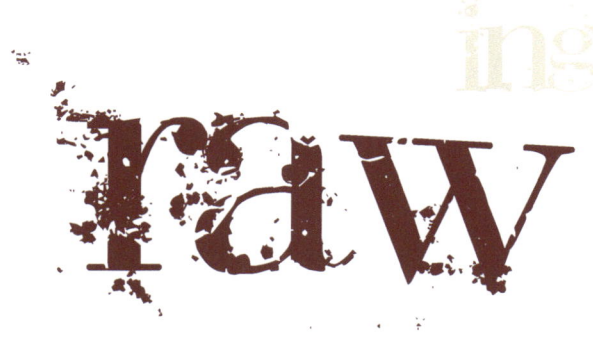

raw ingredients

Iris Morden Ralph Critchlow Angela
Hansen Darryl W Funk Emmy Bouma
Cherie Hanson Jennifer Burrows Mel
Hunt Bonnie Anderson Lynden
Beesley Katherine Upton Tina
Siddiqui Julia Trops Michele Nobel
Yvonne Morrish Carrie Harper Laura
Salisbury Carol Hermesh Gabriel
Dinim Diana Wilkinson TJ Critchlow
Karen Close Diana Creasey-Funk
Angella Goodon Daniel McKellar
Kevin Ade Joyce Dalton Carrol
Spear Craig Warner Aunaray C
Clusiau Rob Zeer Lauren B Wilson
A Woodside Design Gallery
Our Fabulous viewers

Okanagan Erotic Art Show 2009
A Woodside Design Gallery Kelowna
June 1 - 30 2009

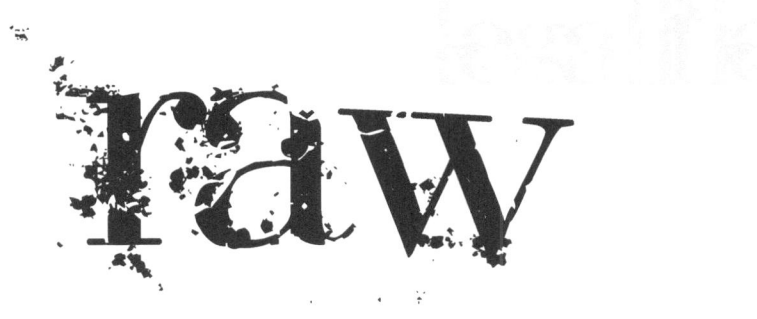

ISBN 978-0-9813363-7-4

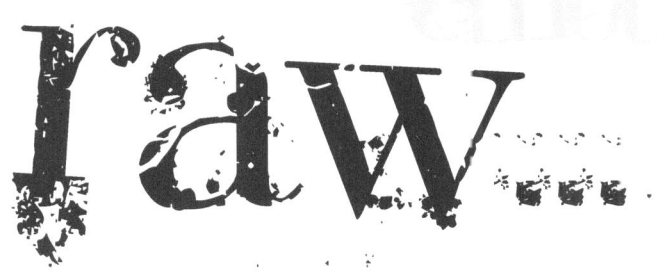

raw... *emotions*

well, girls, another step on the way.

This catalogue
is dedicated to Angie and Lauren
without whom
the first erotic show
would not have happened -
and,
those glasses of wine didn't hurt either.

And to Alisso,
who has the heart and soul
of an adventurer,
I say a heartfelt "Thank you!"

And to Rebekah, the visionary,
without whom
this catalog would not be in existence,
and who is a terrific proof-reader!

Julia

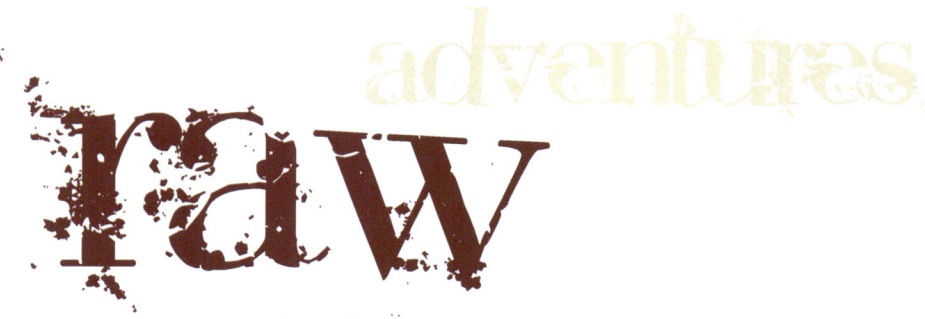

raw

It is the start of an exciting time when we can actually have an annual erotic show in the Okanagan! Raw...whispers 2009 is sure to make some jaws drop while on exhibit through out the month of June. Taking a plunge into the busy downtown core, this years' show is being held at a venue sure to get attention! A Woodside Design GALLERY, is a commercial gallery which supports the talents of local BC Artists.

As owner of the Gallery, and a Kelowna painter myself, I'm always keen to discover new ways to represent and expose the artists of the Okanagan. When submissions began to pour in early this Spring, it reconfirmed once again the level of creative talent we have right here, within our region. I immediately jumped at the chance when asked to host the location of this years' Erotic Art Show.

I recently listened to the advice of Artist, Robert Genn when he wrote about donating as an artist. He mentioned that it's very important to donate your time/money/energy towards something of personal value because it will then benefit yourself in doing so. I have talked to many people who say, when talking about the ideas brought forth by this show, "I still remember when there wasn't a place in Kelowna that would allow 'nude' art". Of course there will always be whispers questioning some of the intimacies of this show and I'm willing and excited to hear all the feedback-- good and, not so good.

Raw…whispers happens to be the theme and title of this year's show and this lets the artist have freedom in discovering a range of possibilities in what erotic can really be –Note the cover image! As an annual show the changing themes from year to year shall challenge both artist and viewer!

Our city has been taking new strides for quite sometime now—there is a younger demographic staying after high-school thanks to UBC-O, our population has reached the point that an 'urban center' is well underway, and, let's face it, who hasn't been into one of the many adult stores in our area. I think that this bit of risqué is healthy for the fun-loving environment in which we live and thrive.

The gallery hosts a contemporary edge of high caliber art and, being in the bustling downtown, I've been joking around with people saying, "Do you think I'll have to paper over the front windows"?! As much as Kelowna is growing, I don't think you'll see quite as much as a jaunt down Davie St. in Vancouver brings to the eyes! Not yet anyways…!

Put your foot forward and make this exhibition a personal and annual occurrence! As a couple, with your girlfriends –a glass of wine will be available and don't be too shocked if the bartender is sporting a trench coat! This is meant to be an evening of fun so have a glass –that way people won't know exactly why you're looking so… rosy cheeked!

Alissa Woodside

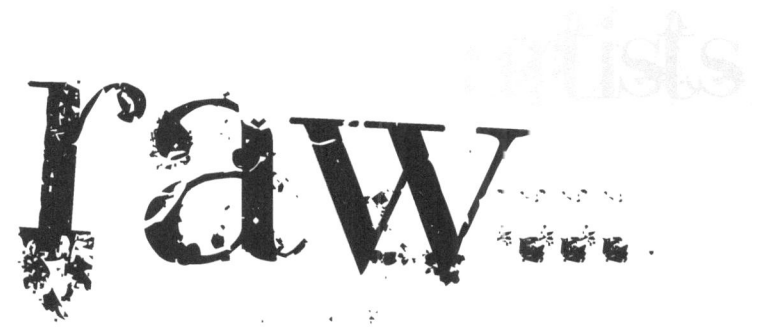

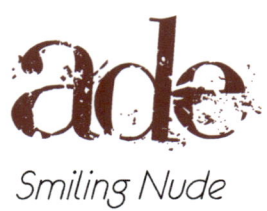

Smiling Nude

This is a woman who is very conscious of herself.

Kevin Ade

Kevin Ade is a tall, dark and handsome young man related to Pablo Picasso through Pablo's relationship with Dora Maar. His work is represented in the Prado, the Hermitage in St. Petersburg and the National Gallery of Canada. His art is a meaningless and inconceivably facile exploration of the sparkling world of boredom.

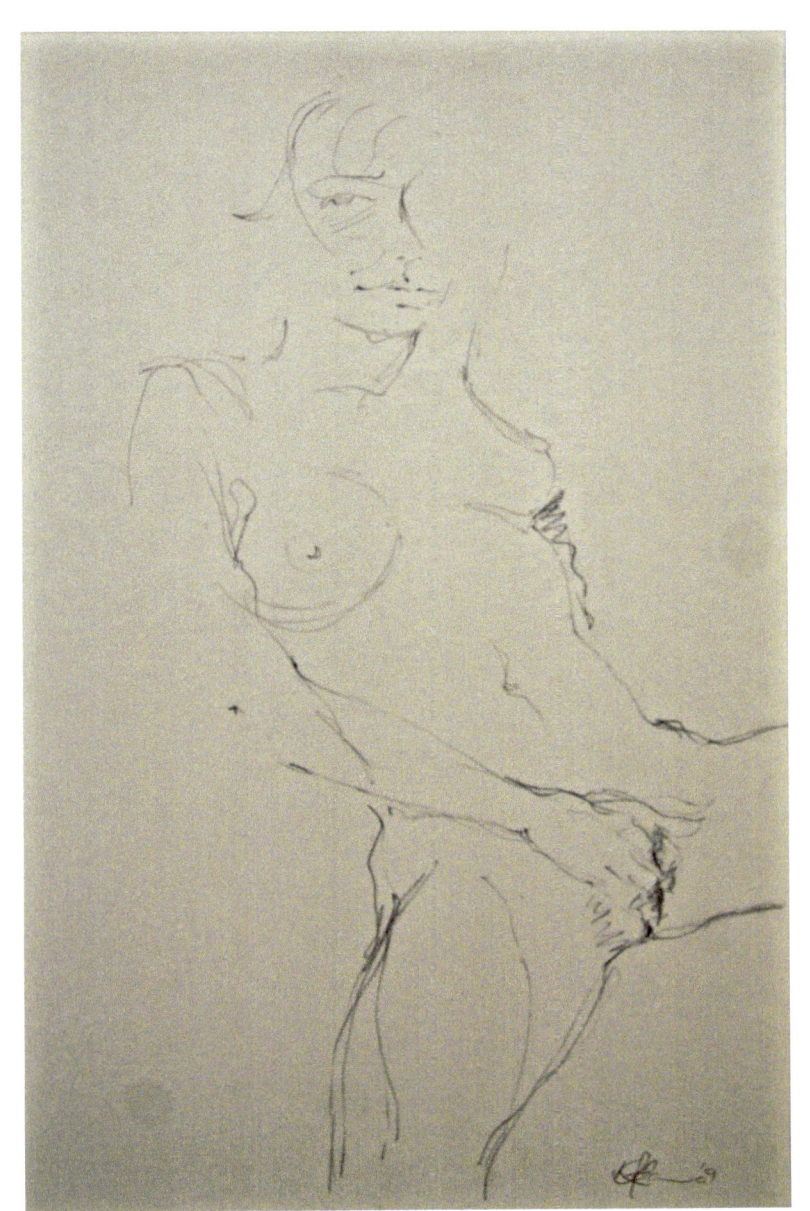

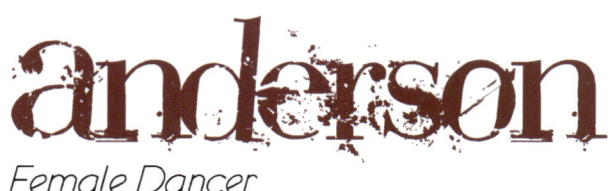

anderson

Female Dancer

Soul printmaking involves drawing directly onto paper that has been placed over ink laden plastic and hand burnished. The drawing is lifted off the ink pad, allowed to dry then the paper is torn, matted, and framed.

Bonnie Anderson

I moved to the Rotary Centre for the Arts in 2002 from my studio on Sexsmith Rd. in Kelowna. This is where I made pottery and taught about clay and its possibilities. I began to have an incredible yearning to pick up a paint brush and paint again. What else could I expect being surrounded by all kinds of painter personalities and their varied mediums? Women are the main subject of my figurative work and women with a good sense of humour are those who appreciate and purchase it.

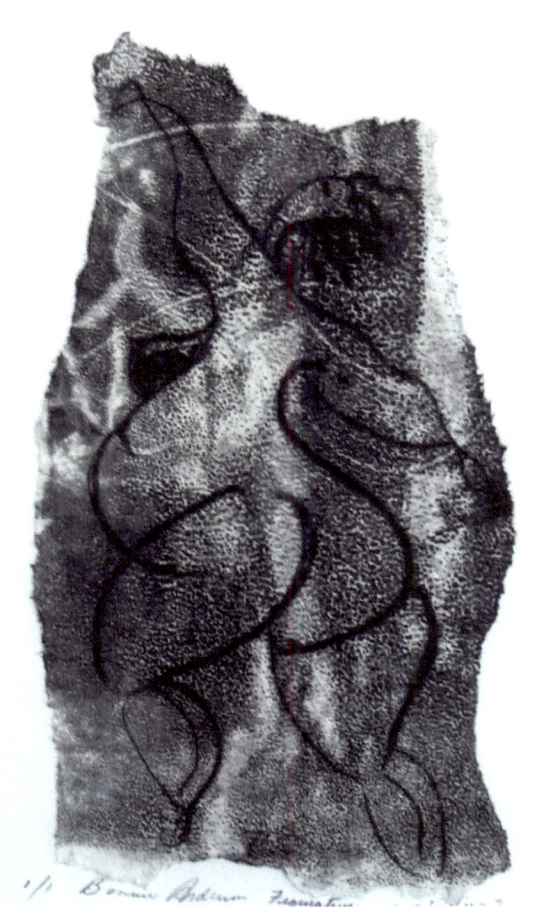

1/1   Bonnie Anderson   Frustration

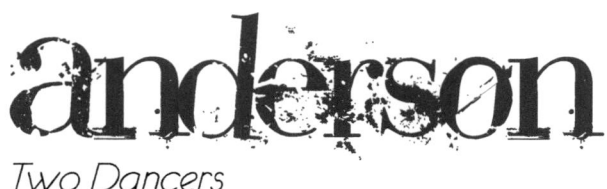

anderson

Two Dancers

This clay piece has been fired in a kiln five times and includes biscuit, under glaze, glaze, lustre and gold firing techniques.

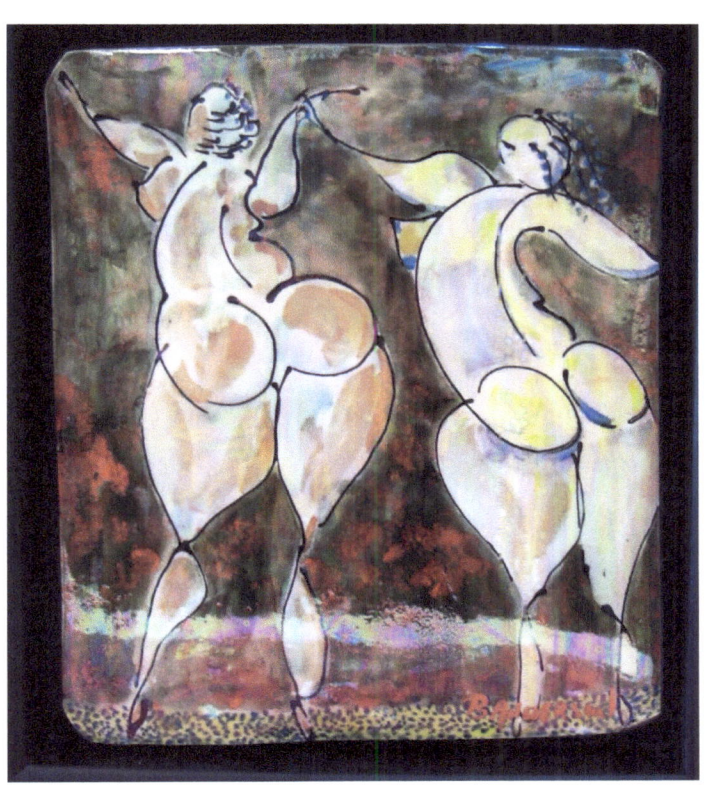

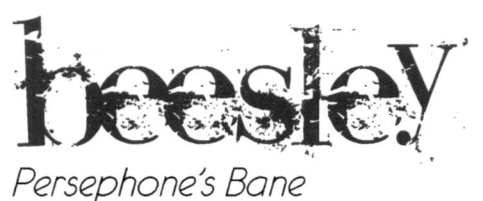

Persephone's Bane

Based on the primal Greek myth of death and rebirth where Persephone was abducted by Hades, kept captive in the underworld and only allowed above ground at the behest of the other Gods.

Lynden Beesley

Lynden Beesley was raised in Surrey, England. She developed a love for art from an early age. In 1975 Lynden she immigrated to Canada with her husband and two daughters. For twenty years, she practiced podiatry in Winnipeg. In 1997, Lynden moved to Eastern Ontario to formally pursue a career in art at Queen's University. She graduated in 2001 with a Bachelor of Fine Arts specializing in printmaking and sculpture. Lynden is an interdisciplinary artist based in the Okanagan. Currently she is past president of the Kelowna Sculptors Network Society, Canadian delegate to FIDEM, a docent at the Kelowna Art Gallery for the "Art in Site" program and a member of the Ars Longa artists group with whom she exhibits regularly.

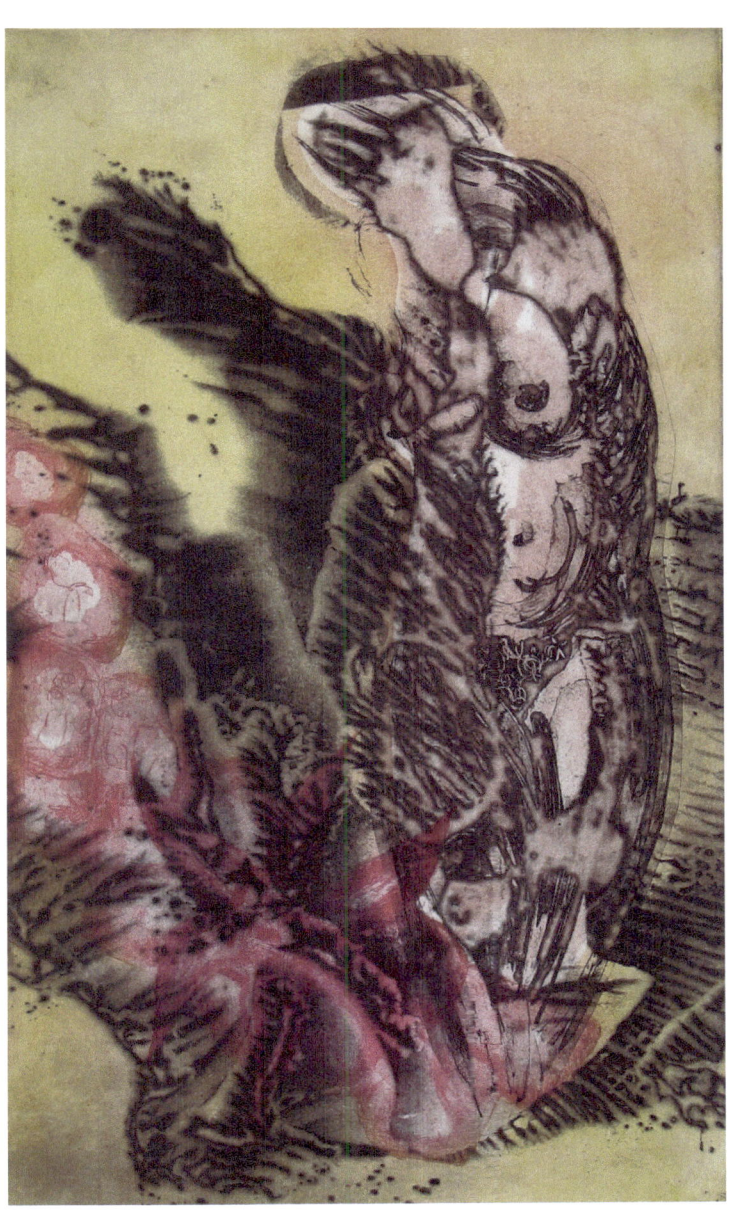

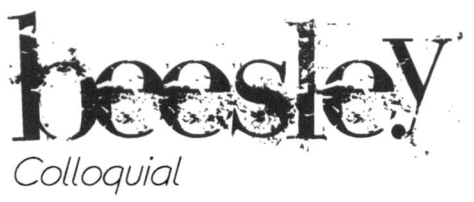

Colloquial

An alabaster sculpture repeats the forms seen in the print and is based on the love poem of the same name by Rupert Brooke.

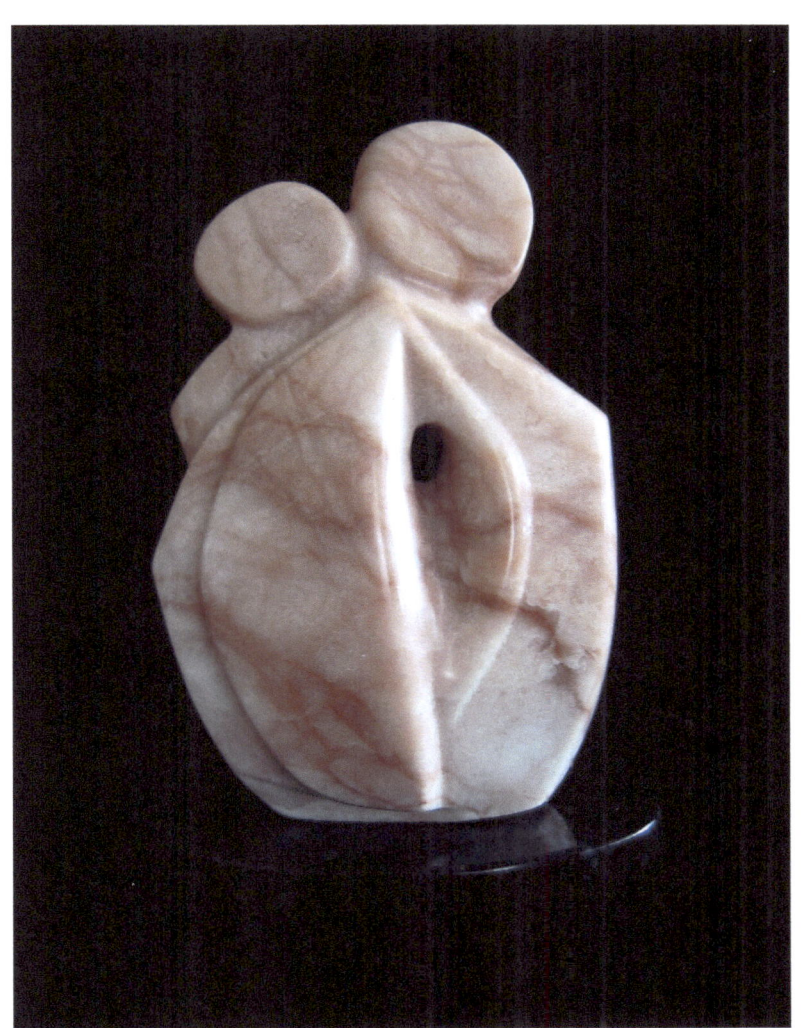

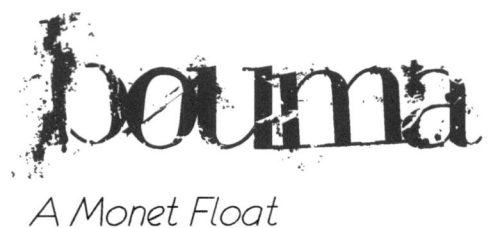

bouma

A Monet Float

Emmy Bouma

Born in Belgium . She came to Canada in 1951 and made her home in many different parts of Canada. She studied art where there was an opportunity e.g. Sheridan school of Design in Mississauga, Donevan Collegiate in Ottawa Over the years she volunteered at the K.A.G. as assistant curator and also volunteered at KADAC. (now Arts council of the central Okangan). Her paintings have been described as realistic impressionism. She usually starts her paintings by applying colour at random to the canvas and then proceeds from there. The final painting becomes strictly imaginary. She likes collage and colours all her own materials for that purpose.

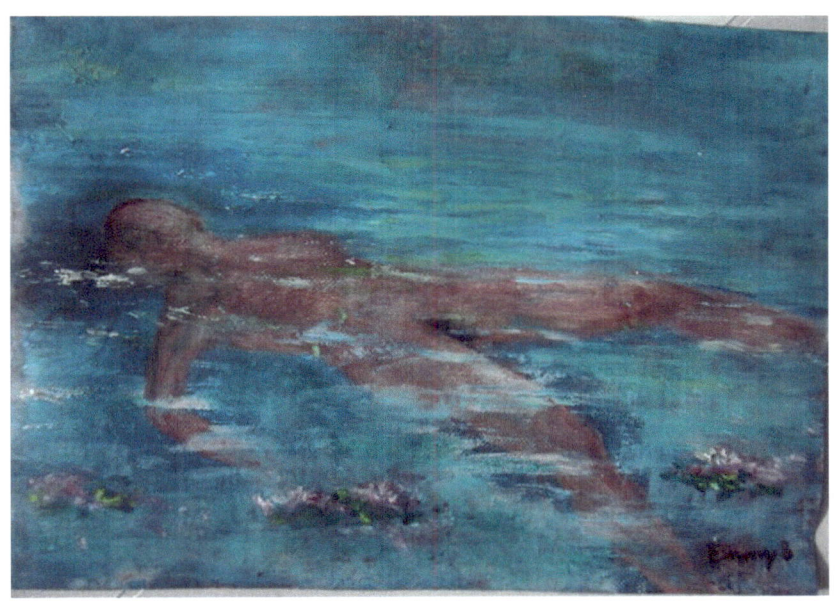

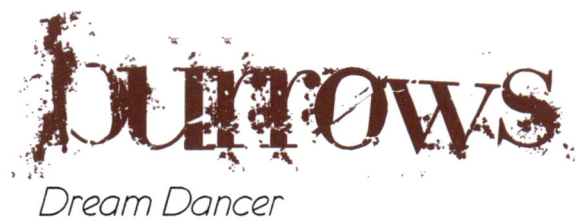

Burrows

Dream Dancer

I find tremendous spirit in the freedom of what isn't precisely controlled or tightly defined. For me, painting is playing with possibilities........and enjoying the intimate conversation between me and the image as it emerges.

Jennifer Burrows

I was born and raised in Montreal and hold degrees from Concordia University and Simon Fraser University. Five years working with large corporations in Montreal and Vancouver came before a twenty-eight year career as a full-time educator in Vernon. At long last I now have time to develop and express my inner artist.

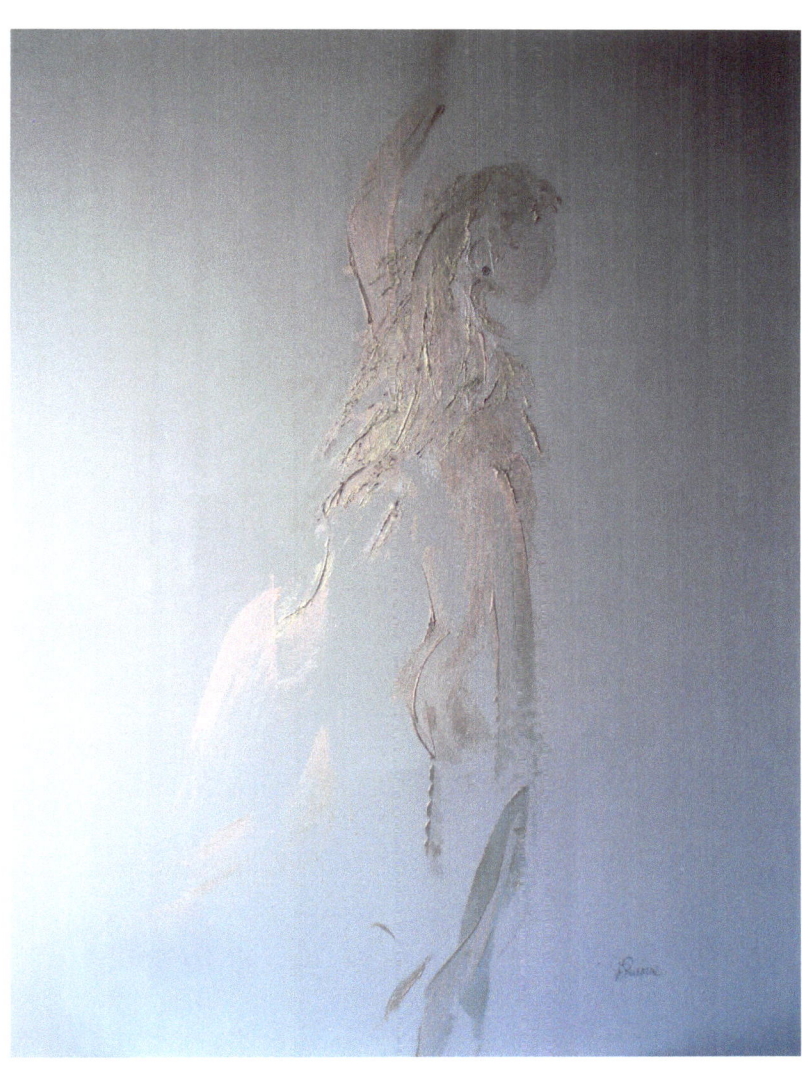

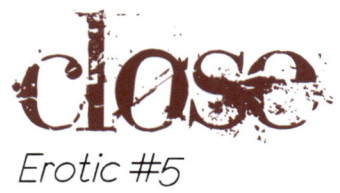

Erotic #5

My works are about sensation and energy.

Karen Close

For twenty-seven years I taught English and Art within public and independent school systems. I am a graduate of the University of Western Ontario with a degree in English and Psychology. Concurrent with my teaching career I achieved a Visual Arts Specialist degree in education and was active with community programming for local art galleries and associations. Since February 14, 2008 I have led an enthusiastic group of painters at the Rotary Centre for the Arts. Our challenge is to release and explore creative energy through "spontaneous process painting". Each work is allowed to evolve as a creative event which explores the mysteries of the unconscious mind.

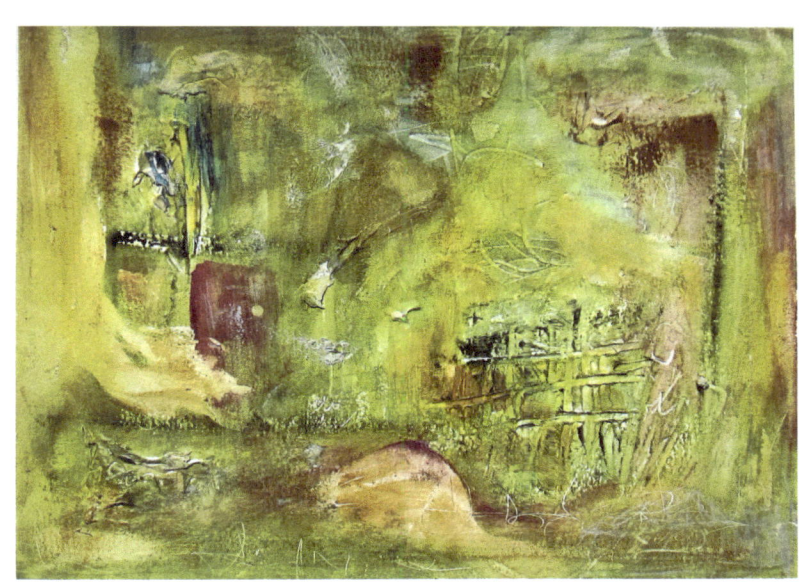

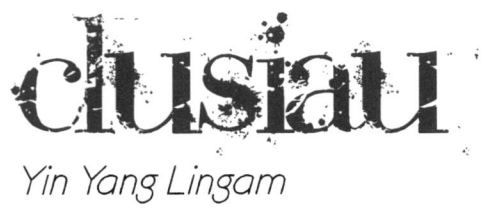

clusiau

Yin Yang Lingam

What is it that you don't understand? It's a fucking painting

Aunaray C Clusiau

Growing up in Toronto Aunaray C.Clusiau aka Carol Clusiau was blessed by location to frequent the plethora of art galleries available to her. She graduated from Emily Carr College of Art and Design with a major in film. In 1995 she was accepted into the prestigious Canadian Film Center as a Resident Director and screenwriter. Retired from film directing, she is happy to be living away from the big city, in the beautiful Okanagan where she sometimes designs and sells jewelry at the farmers market and has recently taken up painting.

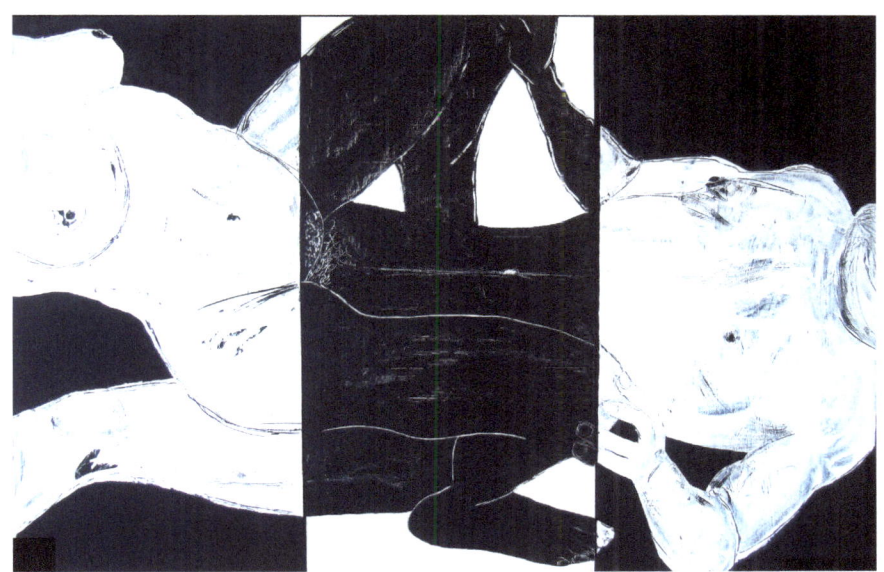

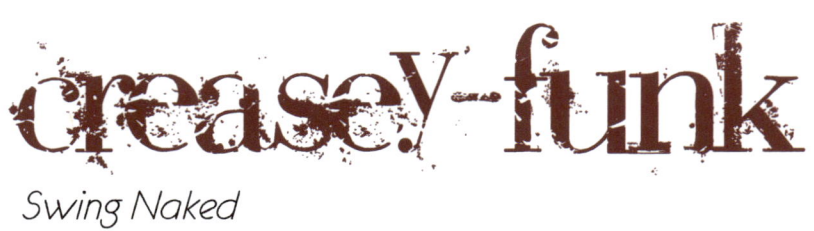

Swing Naked

"Big Fun!"

Diana Creasey-Funk

Originally from Alberta, I moved to the Okanagan in 1986. Attending Okanagan University College I graduated in 1996 with a "Fine Arts Diploma" with distinction. My work is in a wide variety of mediums, styles and subject matter from multimedia primitive sculptures to realistic images on large canvases to this series "Primary Colors".
My works can be found at "Funk tion al" in Kelowna and at "The Barn Gallery" in Oyama. Presently I work from my home studio just outside of Kelowna.

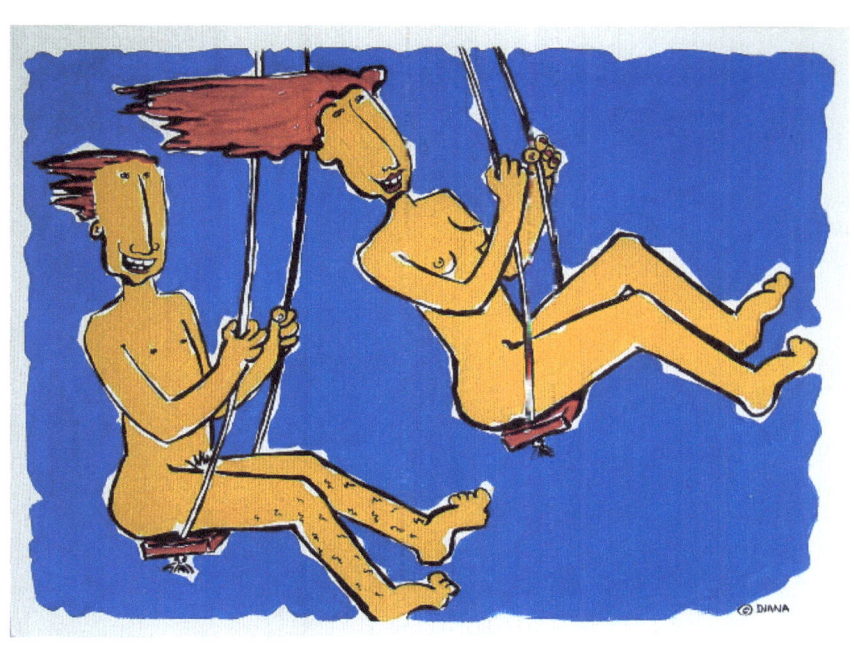

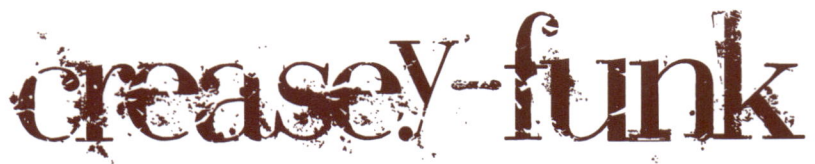

Run Naked

"Well its what we all want to do, isn't it?"

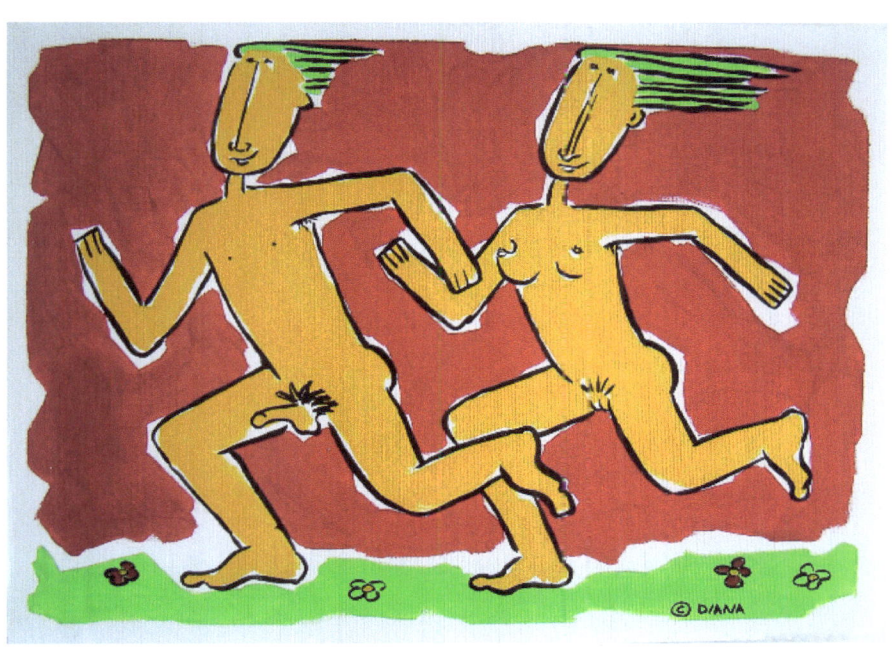

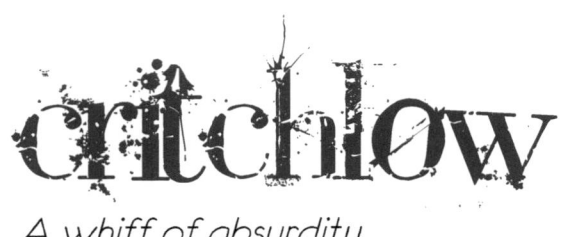

critchlow

A whiff of absurdity

*when an artistic effort takes on a life of
its own it is sometimes for its own good*

Ralph Critchlow

*Grew up on the prairies. Great stuff! Many long winter days
and nights with little to do other than attempt something
artsy. University of Manitoba for awhile. Grew to enjoy art
and friends, still enjoy art and friends. Want to do more. Art
and life should just be a fun thing.*

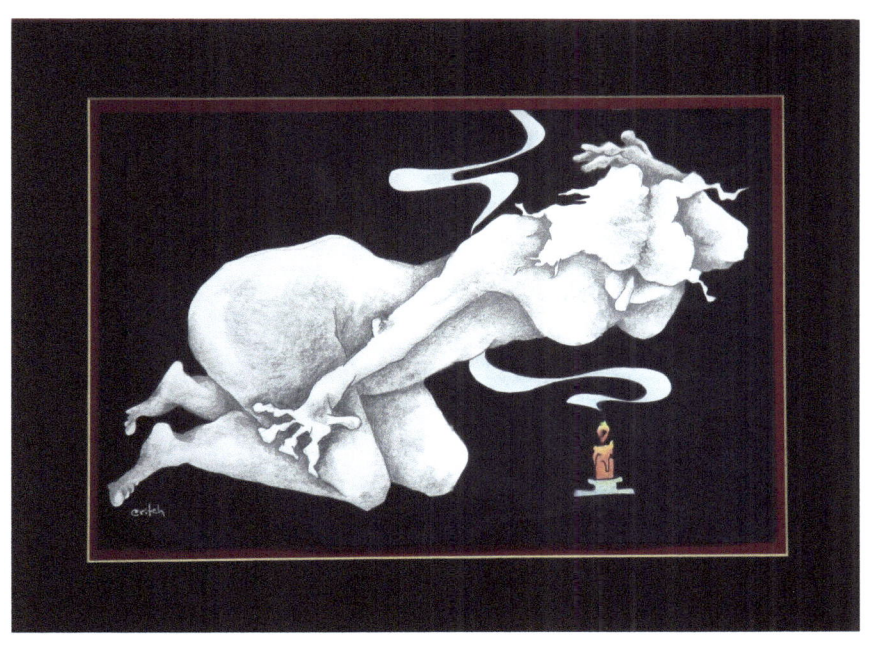

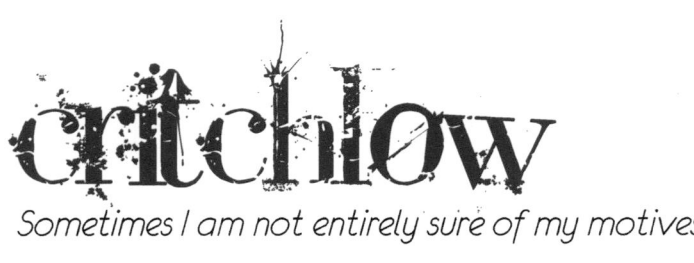

Sometimes I am not entirely sure of my motives

....

*we can often love those with whom we come in
contact and sometimes they love us. Crazy world !*

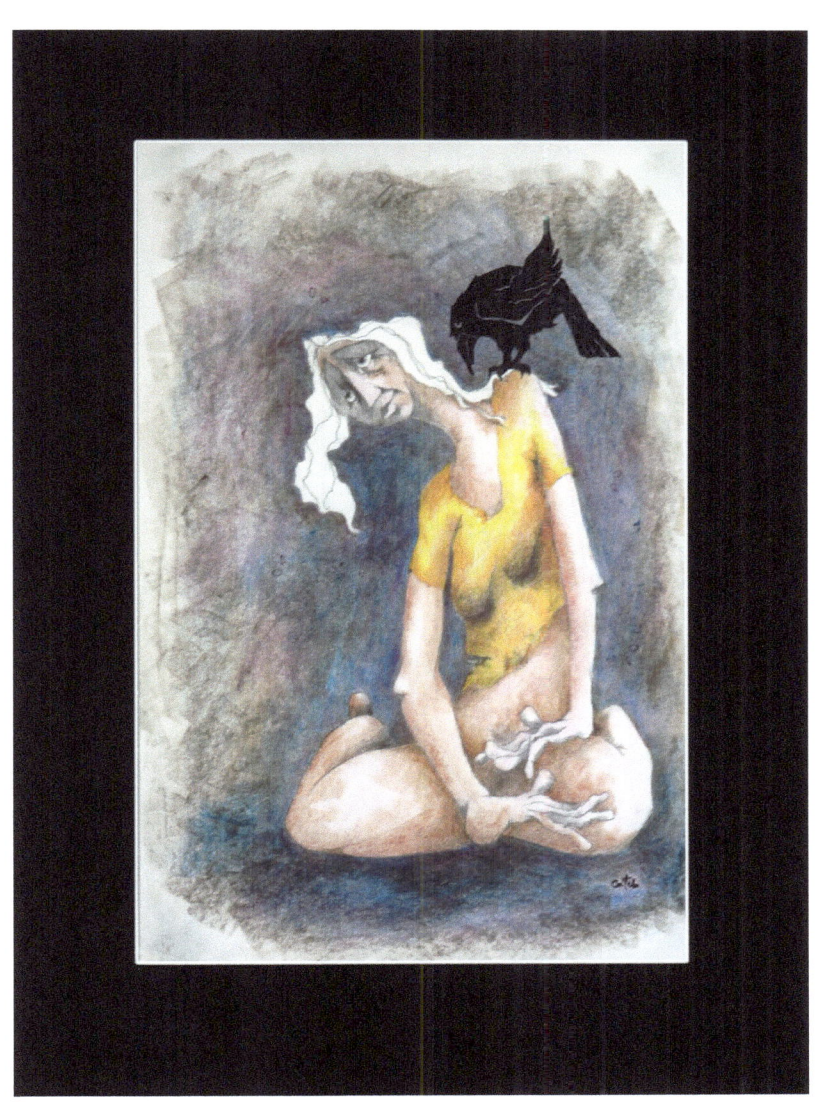

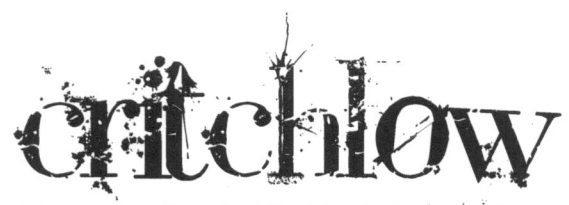

critchlow

*Her expression signified that she was free of second
thoughts about what she was doing, perhaps,
because the light in the window was not for her ...*

*this amusing tragedy could be a quizzical
witticism but the girl does have some attraction*

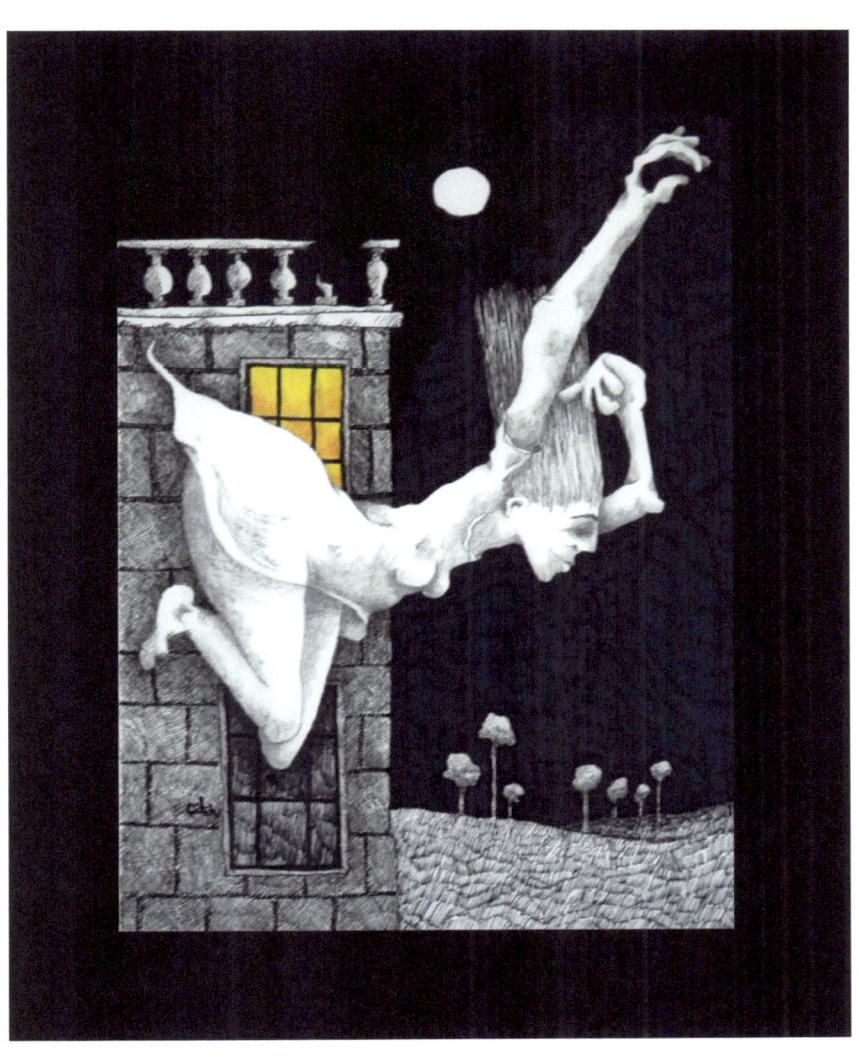

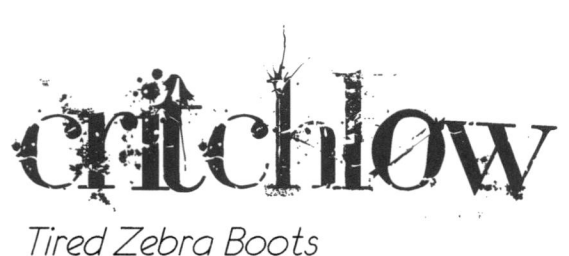

Tired Zebra Boots

This woman lifted her head, looked me in the eye, and said,
'It ain't me who's tired, baby. It's these boots that had a long day.

TJ Critchlow

T.J.Critchlow was born quite a while ago. Did a lot of stuff that, to many, would seem commonplace. And still leads a commonplace existence. But everyday contains something of the superlative.

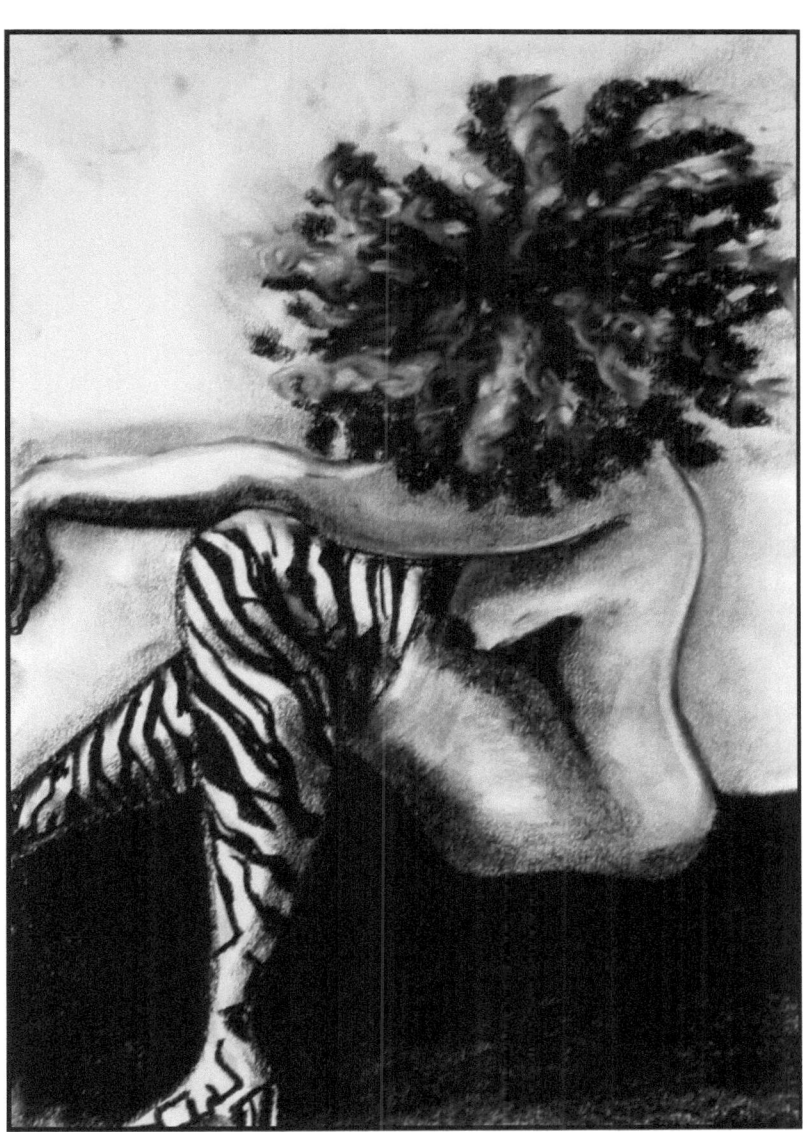

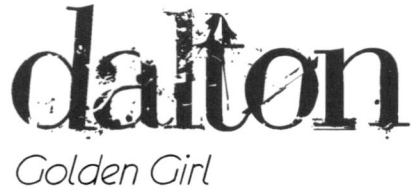

Golden Girl

Joyce Dalton

My lifelong interest in art has now morphed into a retirement project. I have attended children's classes at the Winnipeg School of Art, under L.L.Fitzgerald, and as an adult, evening classes under George Swinton. Later the Ottawa School of Art and Nepean Visual Art Center, working in oils and water-colours. I have participated in several shows, member of Source of Art in Ottawa, and current member of Livessence and Company of Artists. I enjoy working in colour, oils and pastels, painting figures, portraits and landscapes.

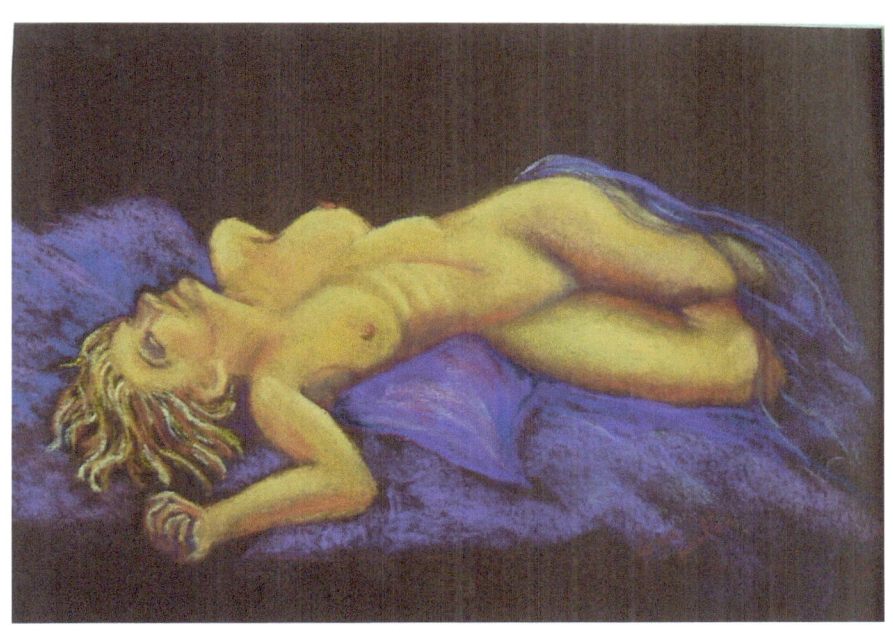

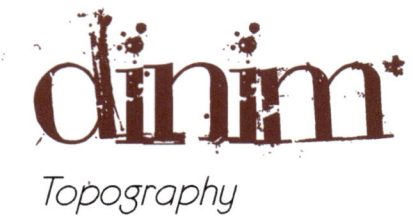

Topography

Shapes of arousal across eons.

Gabriel Dinim

At the age of 21, I put my camera down because the world around me had become a sheet of photopaper. Twenty years later the death of a very dear friend made me mortal. I picked up my camera again (a large format camera this time), my passion was mature enough that it did not insulate me from the world, on the contrary; what better way to live the short life of a mortal than to consciously look at beauty, all beauty. I avoided nudes for a very long time, I found it difficult to offer an original viewpoint in such a well covered genre. I finally screwed up my courage and here are some of progeny.

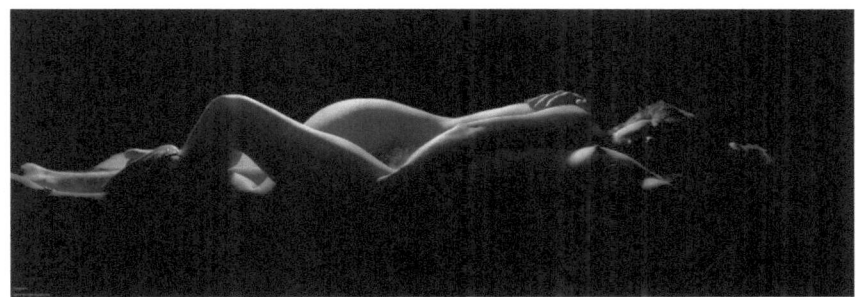

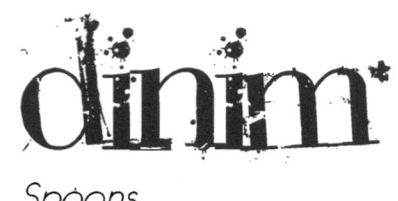

Spoons

*I wanted to illustrate the fact that intimacy is universal
and that gender is mostly appearance.*

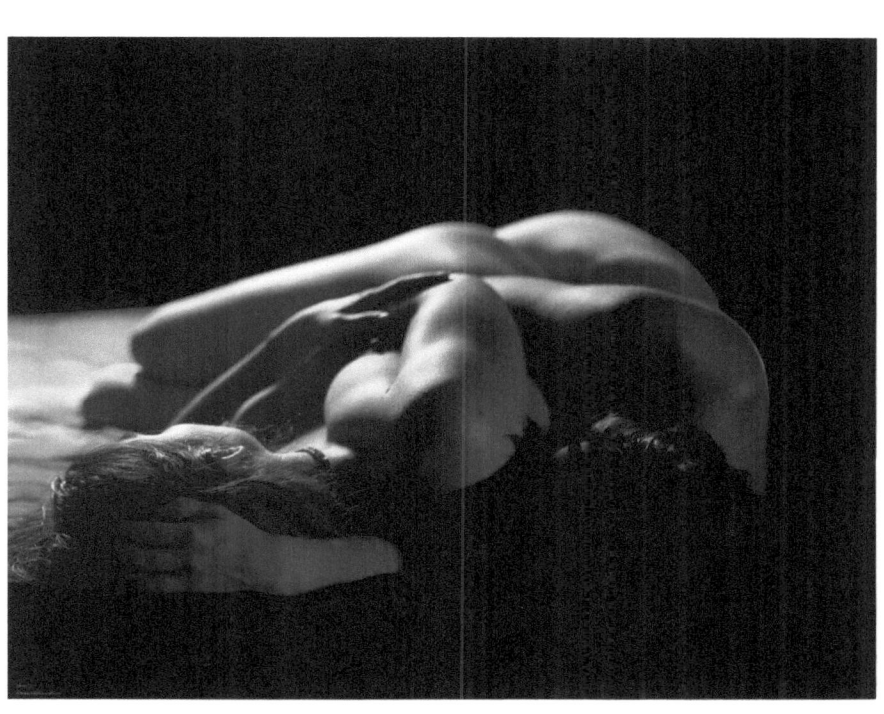

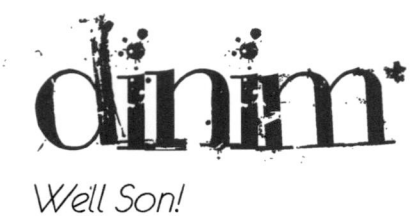

We'll Son!

There are two kinds of men, the wankers, and those who lie about it.

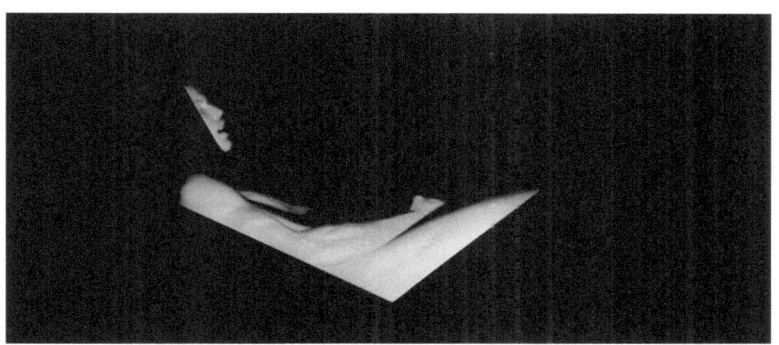

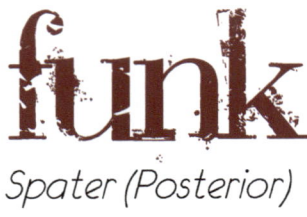

funk

Spater (Posterior)

*In the past my fine art has involved breaking down old
machinery into simple, graphic shapes and colours,
and for this show, I decided to apply the same process to
the female anatomy.*

Darryl W. Funk

*Darryl W. Funk received his BFA in Printmaking from the
Alberta College of Art and Design. During his childhood, his
time was spent reading stories of space and adventure. Children's illustrators like Maurice Sendak and Hans Augusto Rey as
well as Jack Kirby, the "King" of comic books, had a major
impact on his desire to become a children's illustrator. In 2005,
Darryl and his wife Janay moved to Kelowna. A year later, he
started work on the first issue of the children's magazine,
"Zamoof!". In the same year, he illustrated his first children's book
entitled, "Skunky Lunky and Weasel Beasel at Sleepy Hollow
Farm", written by Carol Orr. While enjoying the
opportunity to practice fine art, the majority of his time is spent
raising his daughter Annaliese and illustrating tales of space and
adventure.*

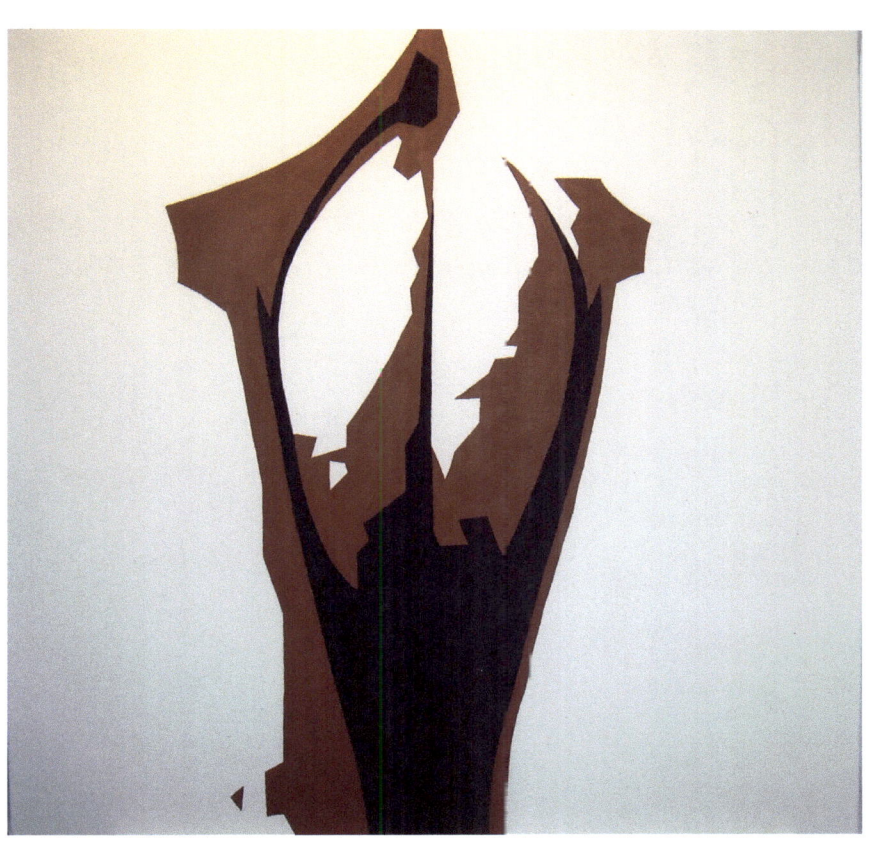

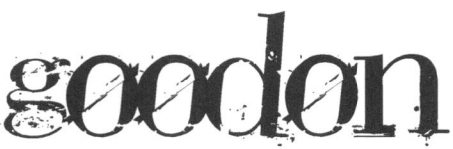

goodon

Colors of the Feminine Splendor 1

What lies beneath are the naked emotions she dares to show the world, her splendour, her spirit

Angella Goodon

Angella Goodon is an emerging abstract artist, currently living and working in Kelowna, BC (Canada). As a young child she was constantly drawing or painting. During her school years she took every art related class possible. In 2006, Angella decided it was time to improve on her self-taught skills and enrol in classes towards a Diploma in Art. In 2008, she graduated with honours. Angella currently works in acrylics but enjoys all mediums. And while she does a lot of her work on paper, canvas is her preference. Canvas gives her the freedom to create more depth. By employing bold lines and vibrant color, she creates art that leaves an open interpretation..

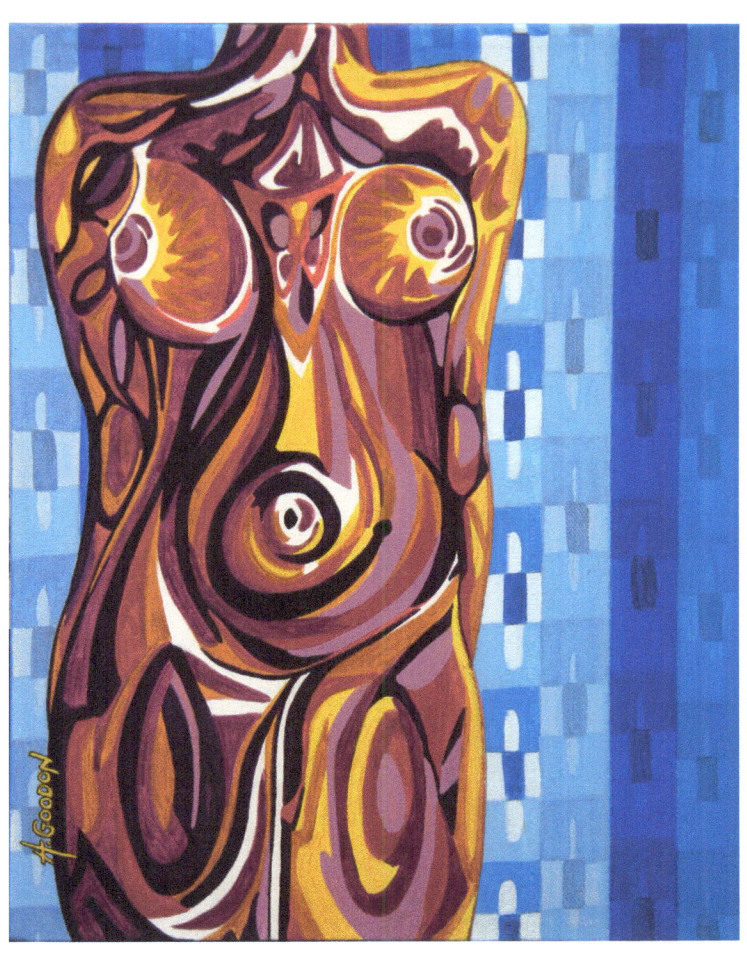

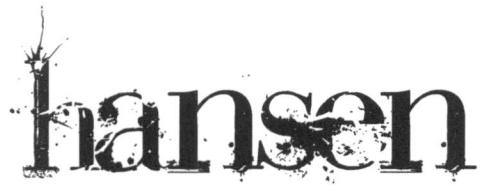

...to the touch #3

*The reliefs are meant to draw the viewer
in close and entice a touch or caress -
just as a lover might do - are you willing?*

Angela Hansen

*Kelowna artist and highschool art instructor, Angela Hansen, is a
graduate of the Emily Carr Institute of Art and Design with a degree
in Communications Design. Angela is primarily a figurative artist
working mostly in 2D mediums in the past, however an interest in
exploring 3D mediums is her interest at present. This artist is inspired
by colour and textures and using mediums in unusual applications, for
instance mixing plaster castings and encaustic waxes. She is always
interested in learning new techniques and mediums. Angela resides in
Kelowna with her husband and their new son.*

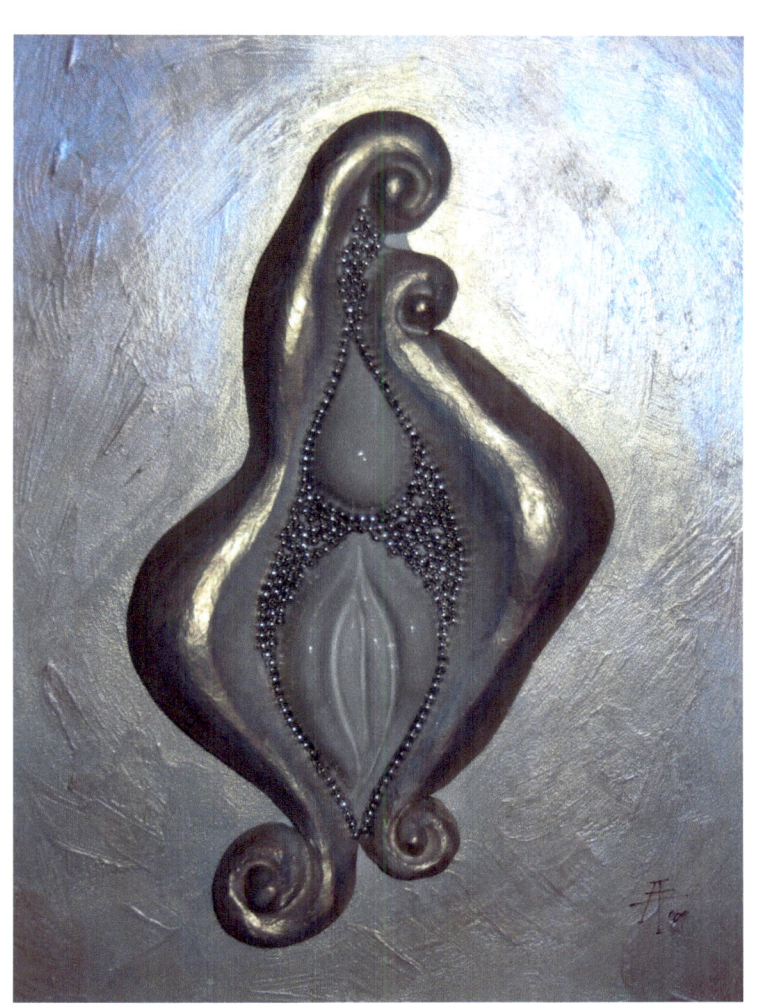

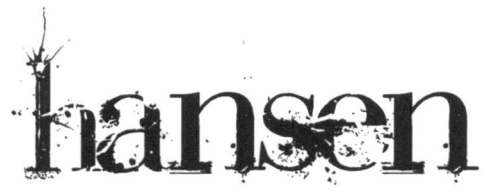

hansen

...to the touch #2

*The reliefs are meant to draw the viewer
in close and entice a touch or caress -
just as a lover might do - are you willing?*

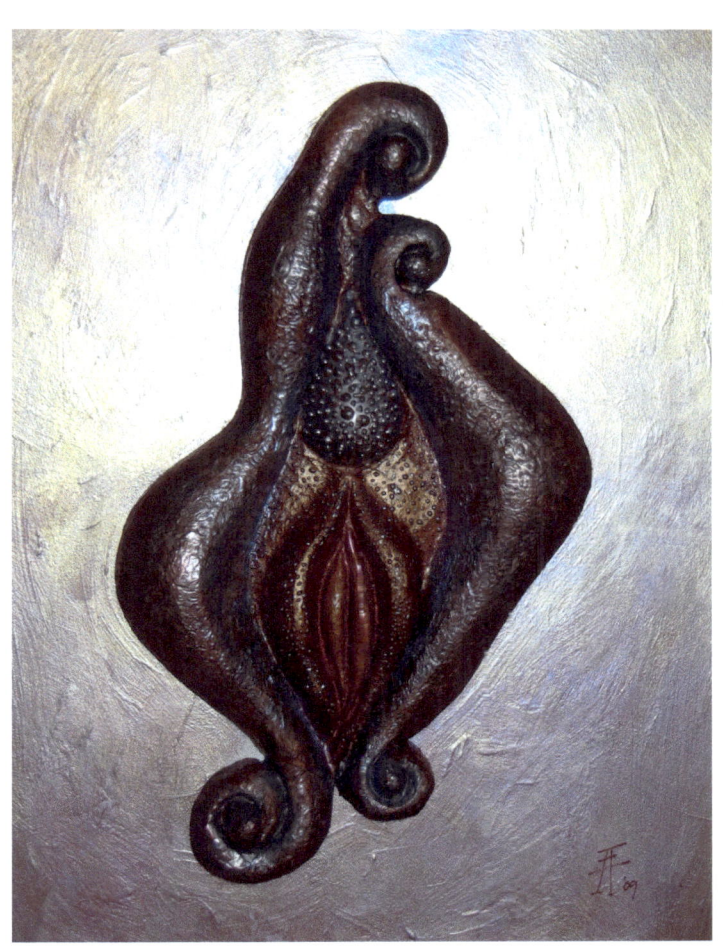

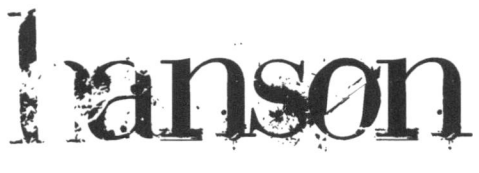

Literate Nude #2

*She is twisting, holding her feet and has that far off look
women get when they take a break from reading nude
and break into yoga.*

Cherie Hanson

*Cherie Hanson is an internationally exhibiting and prize winning
artist. Her works have been juried into shows in Chicago;
Toronto,,Ferrar, Italy; Florence, Italy. She has been selected for
shows in the Kelowna Art Gallery (Women and Souls), the
Kamloops Art Gallery, the Summerland Art Gallery, the
Alternator Gallery and Gallery Vertigo. She is currently
preparing for a curated group show at the Steighaus Gallery in
Vienna, Austria in May, 2009. Her digital work has been
selected for four CD covers, five book jackets and an
anthology cover.*

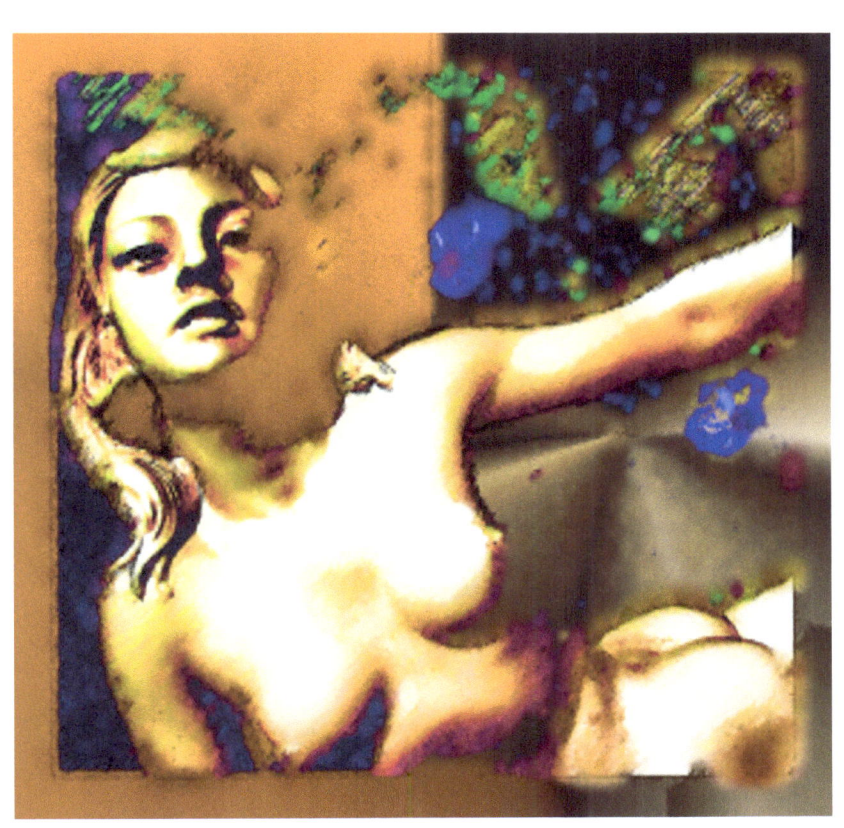

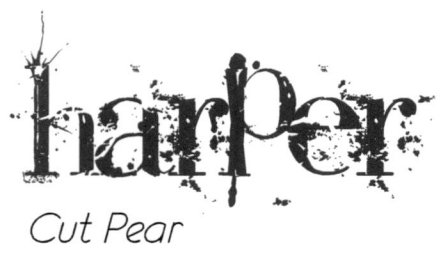

Cut Pear

One day, while taking pictures of cut fruit, I discovered that the pale flesh: moist and delicate, and the center: where eternal life is stored, were intensely female.

Carrie Harper

Carrie Harper studied Fine art, majoring in Textiles and metal smithing, at The Alberta College of Art and Design from 1991-1993. After returning to her childhood home of Kelowna in 2001, from Alberta, returned to creative studies in digital graphic design. From Carrie's perspective, art is the experience of expression rather than a slotting into specific technique or subject matter. She believes that good art stirs personal, soulful meaning and most often does not match your decor. Carrie Harper draws deeply from her experiences of growing up at her family's Okanagan Mission acerage and winery (one of the first three started in the Okanagan).

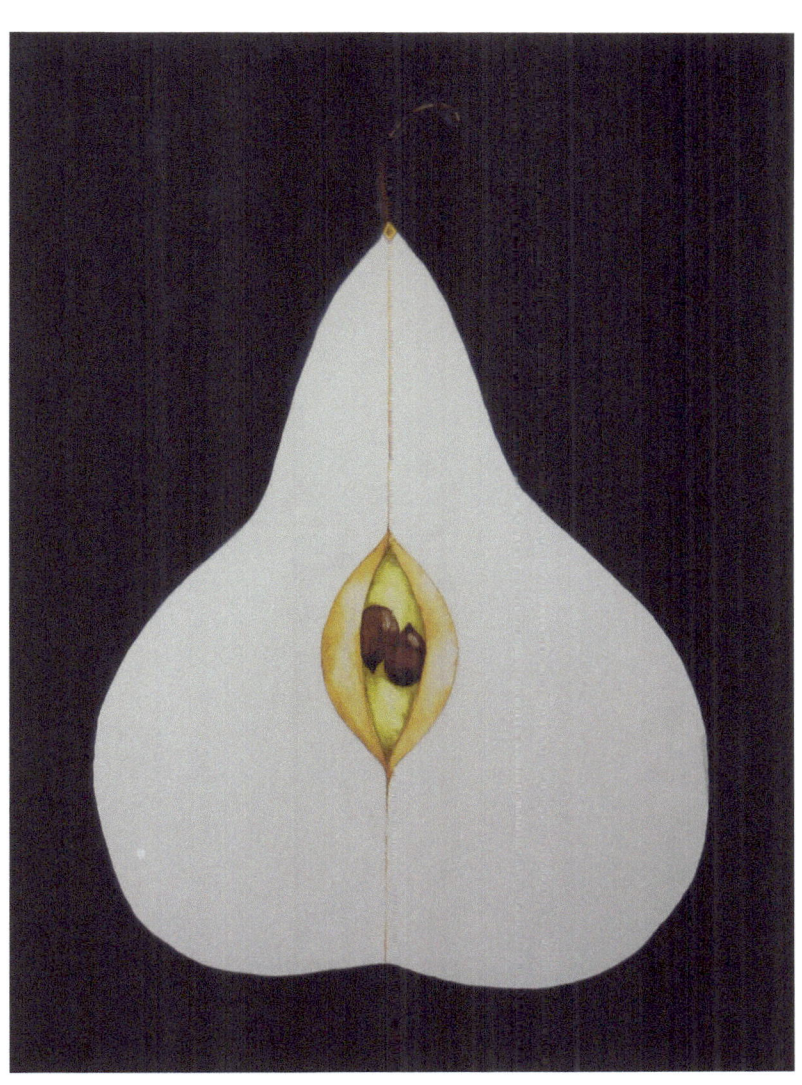

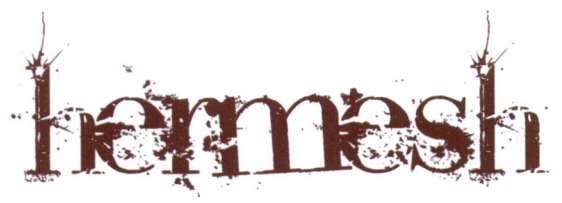

Darkness in a well lit room...

Focusing on erotic vulnerability that speaks in Raw.....whispers....

Carol Hermesh

*Carol Hermesh began exploring the digital world by photo-
graphing her husbands sculpture. The work soon evolved into
combining models and still life photographs in photoshop.
Using a variety of mediums she now uses her photographs in
many various ways by creating photomontages, linocut prints,
photo transfers and portraits. Her work can be found
throughout the Okanagan Valley and online.*

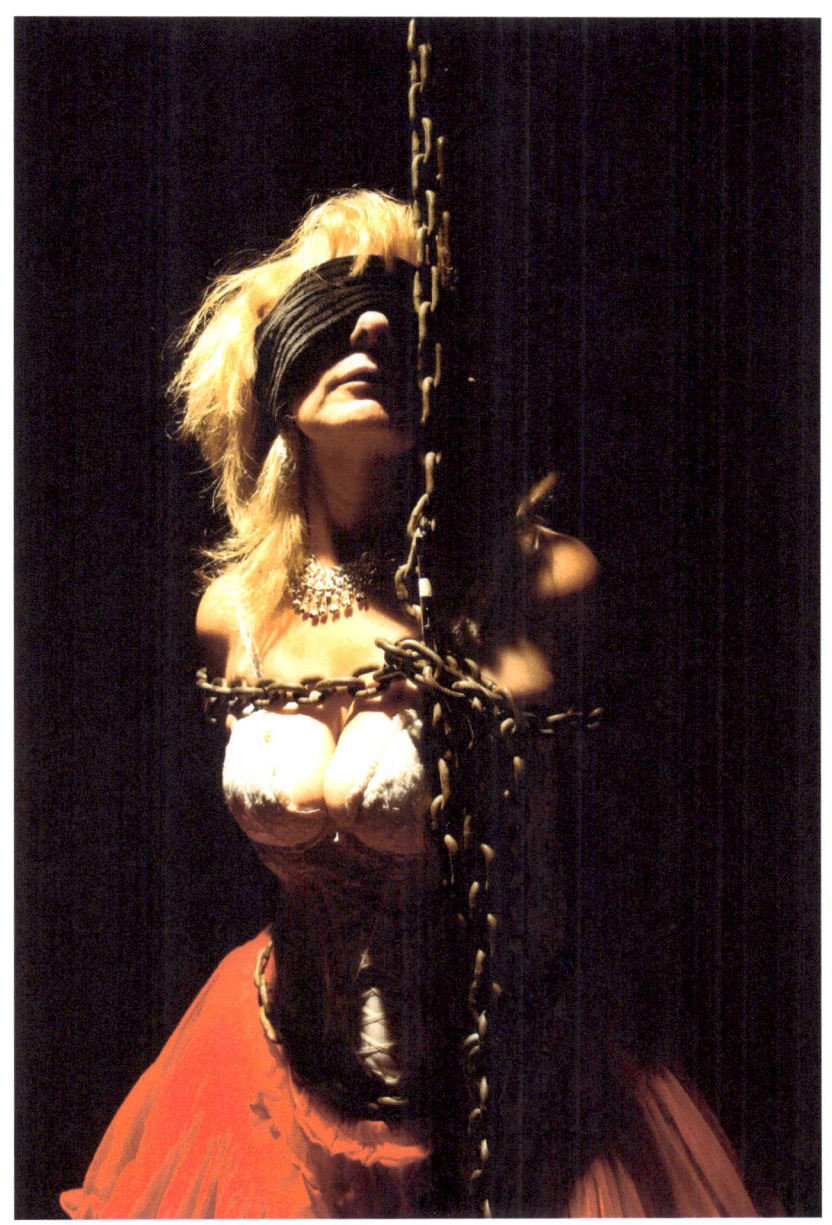

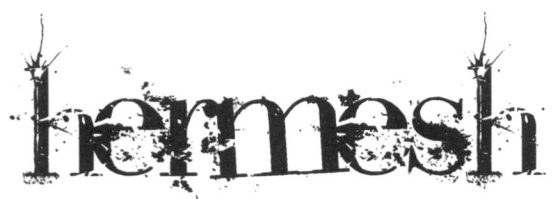

An exact position in a well lit room...

Focusing on erotic vulnerability that speaks in Raw......whispers....

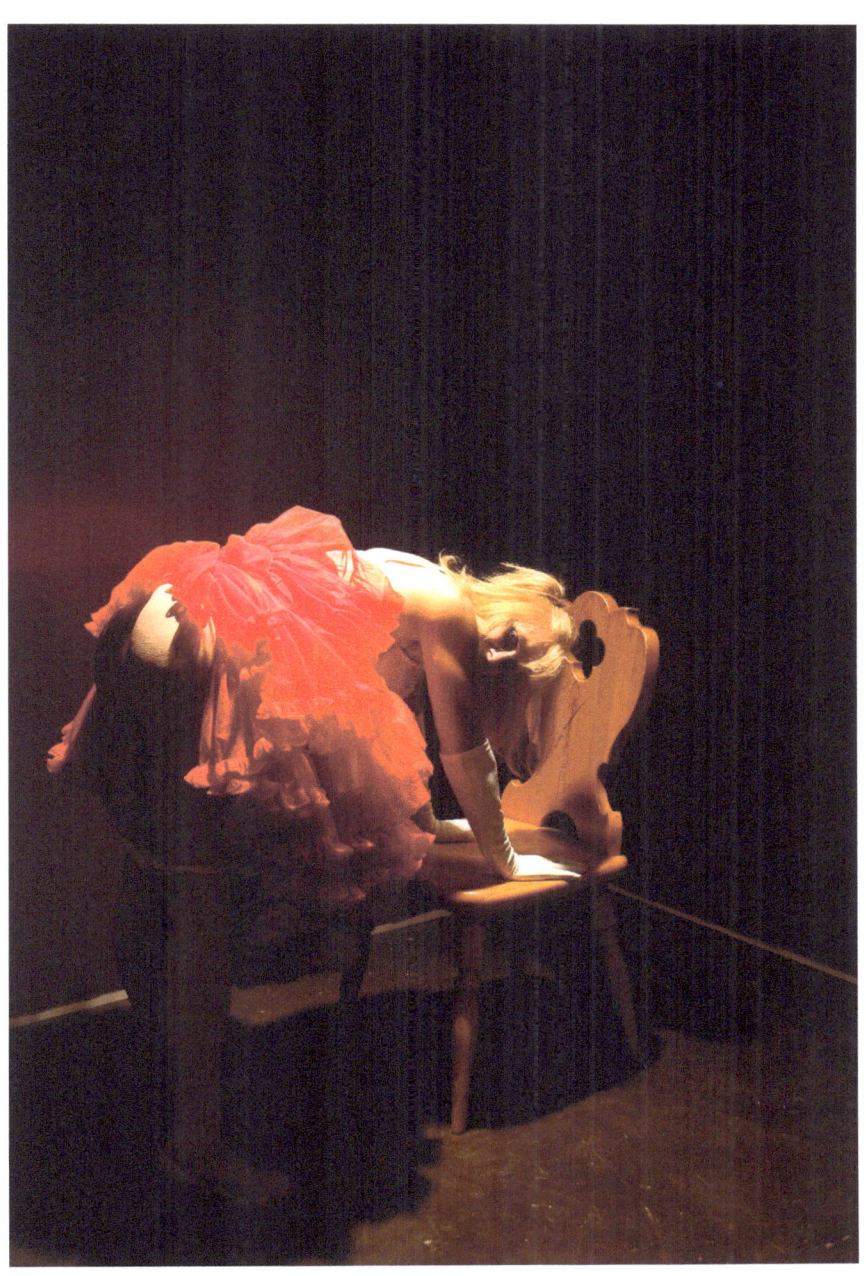

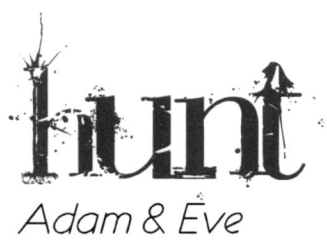

Adam & Eve

Adam and Eve are separate yet united, and already surrounded by defining concepts.

Mel Hunt

Mel Hunt has been living, teaching, and creating in the Okanagan for the last 15 years. A more extensive collection of realistic and abstract works is displayed in the Rotary Centre for the Arts, Studio 112.

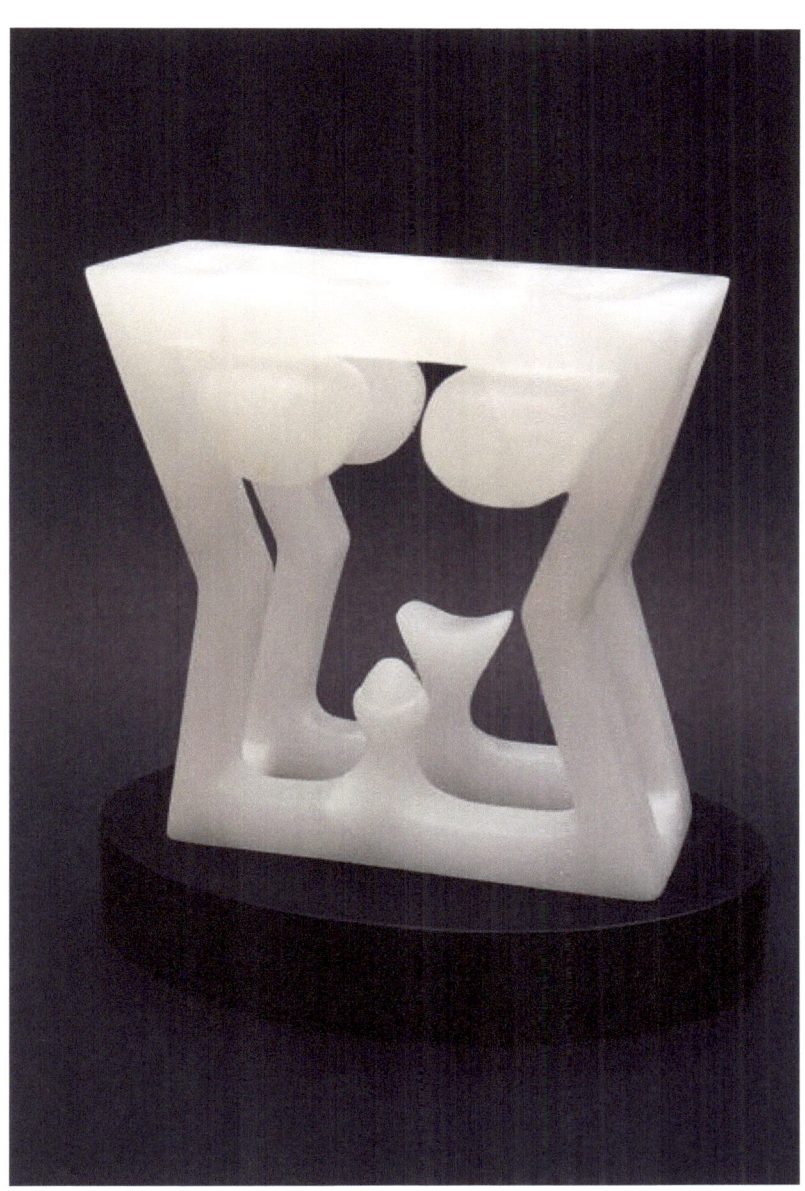

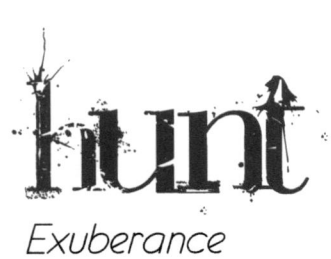

Exuberance

This 'Pink Lady' is just herself!

Mel Hunt

Mel Hunt has been living, teaching, and creating in the Okanagan for the last 15 years. A more extensive collection of realistic and abstract works is displayed in the Rotary Centre for the Arts, Studio 112.

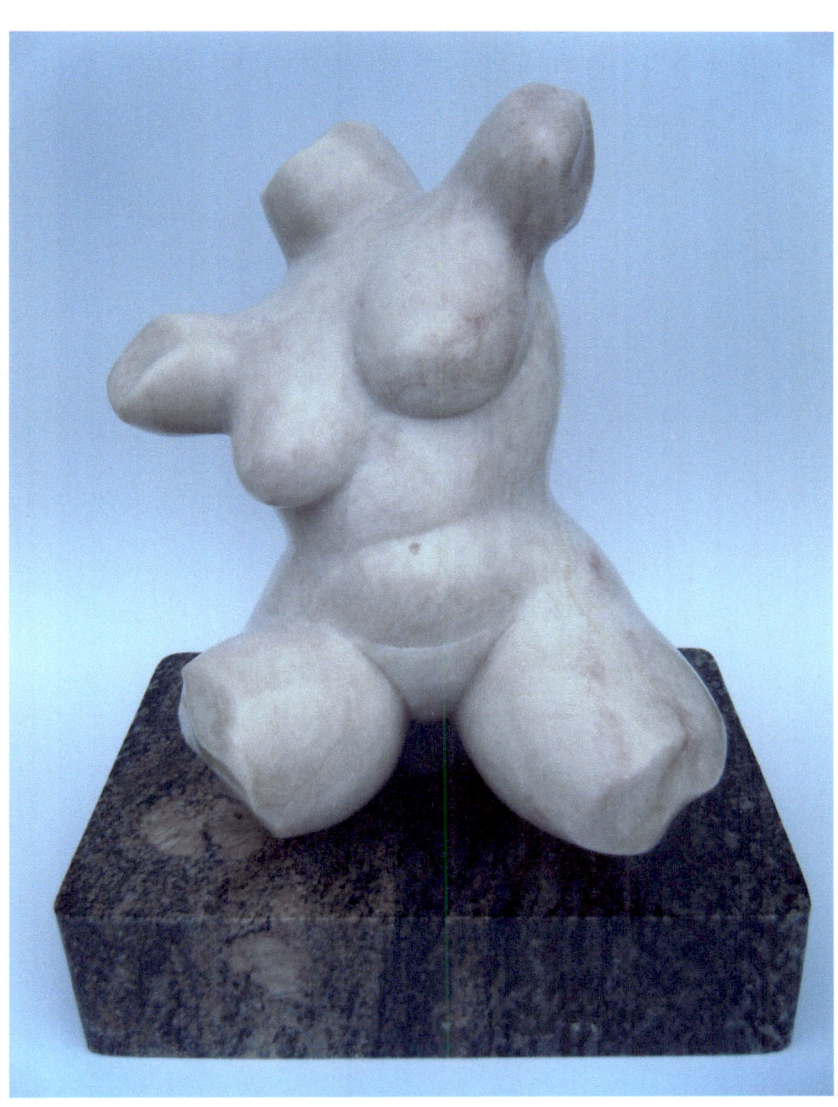

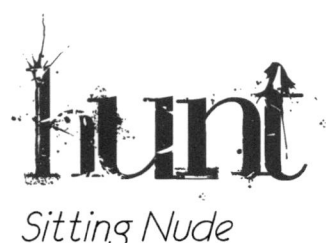

Sitting Nude

Feeling free just to ponder things.

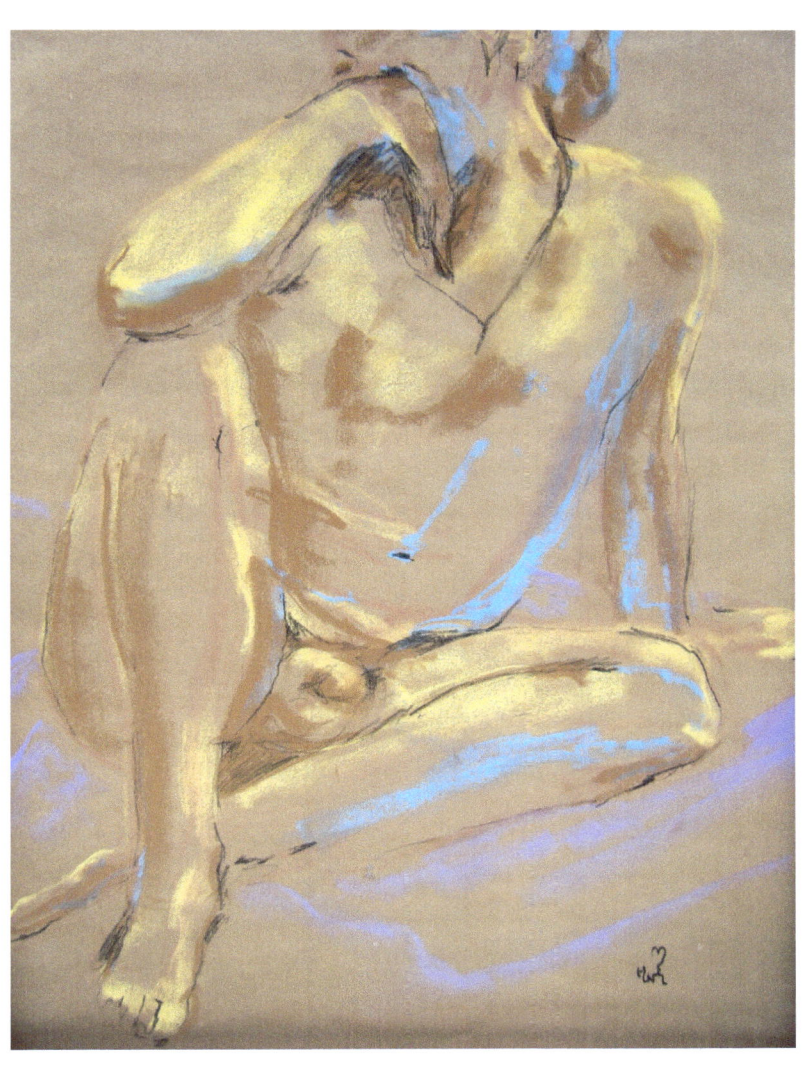

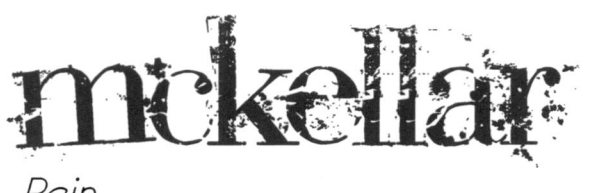

Rain

I paint form and express emotion through colour and texture.

Daniel McKellar

Born in Northen British Columbia, Daniel McKellar is a self taught artist. Drawing since he could hold a pencil, he has always been facinated by the human body and mind. Moving to Vancouver in 1994 to study acting, he worked on various feature film and television productions before moving to Kelowna in 2006 to start a new adventure. He recently had his first art showing in the 2009 U8 exhibit and sold his first painting opening night. He works mainly in oils and acrylics with realistic and abstract properties.

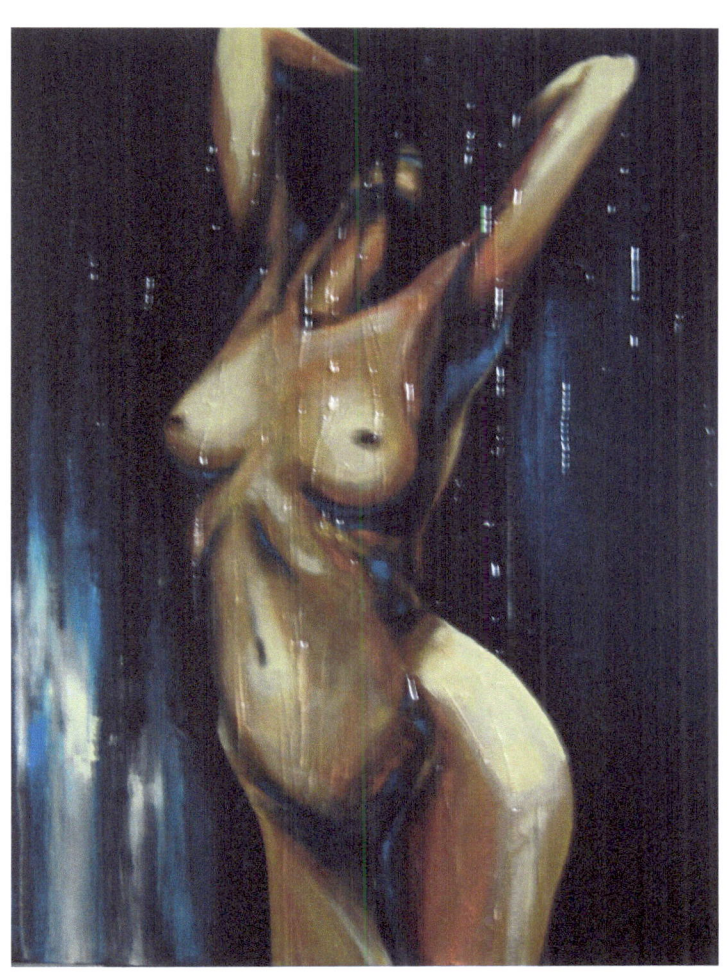

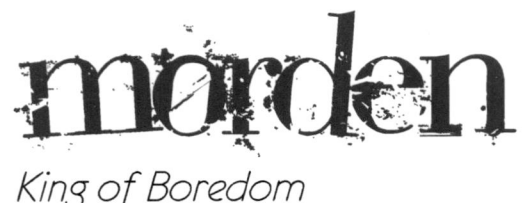

morden

King of Boredom

Society thinks daily life is boring. Life is erotic,
live it naked, tame the boar.

Iris Morden

Iris Morden hopscotches through the arts community with
her tongue firmly in cheek. With a twinkle in her eye she
creates whimsical, humorous and erotic sculpture with a
shelf life that keeps on giving. The viewer's engagement,
whether friendly or hostile, amounts to Iris as acceptance of
the sculpture's giving message. Her art is meant to elicit a
response and to tittilate and entertain the viewer.

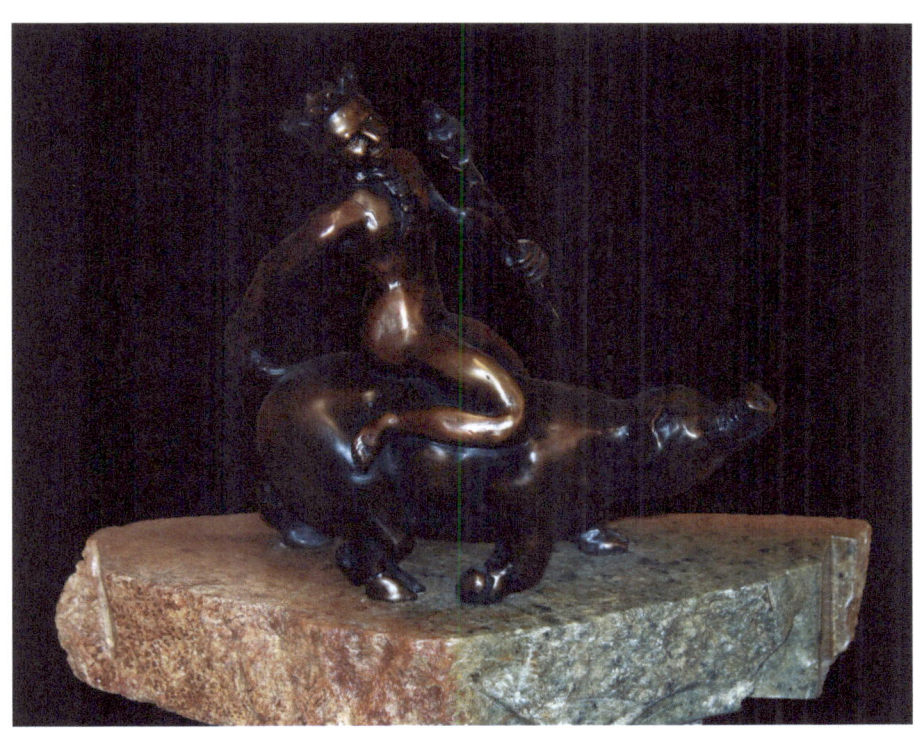

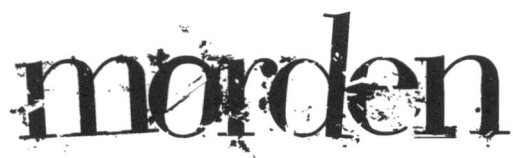

Leaving on a jet plane

Getting satisfaction, should she leave the fig leaf or take it travelling.

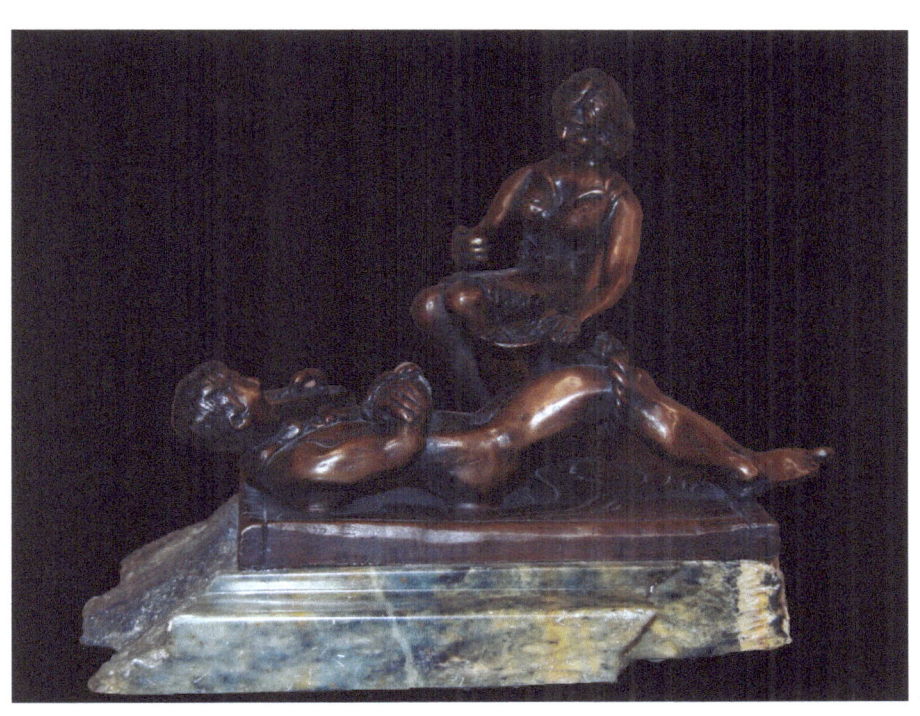

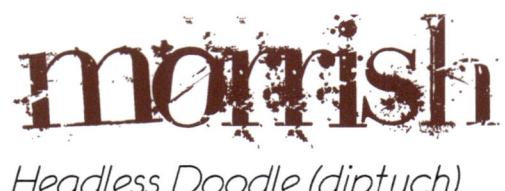

Headless Doodle (diptych)

I love to ink sketch and all from my imagination.
I am never without a sketch book.

Yvonne Morrish

Art is for me and ongoing journey of discovery, developing my skills, pushing myself into new areas of creative expression. The source of my inspiration comes from within and trusting in that inner self, I find an unlimited direction. I love to experiment.

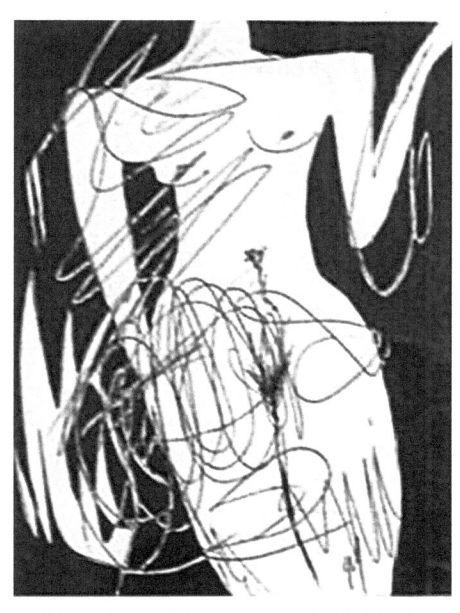

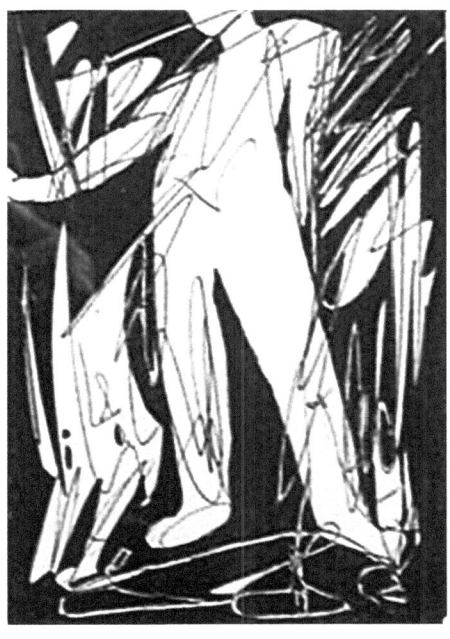

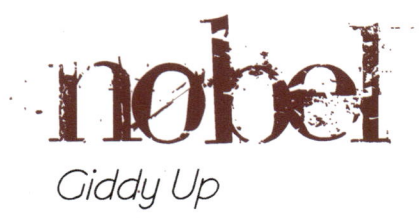

nobel

Giddy Up

Michele Nobel

I am BC born and raised and have been taking photographs since being given a camera at the age of 12. As a freelance photographer what interests me most is using alternative style model photography - fetish; like latex, leather, corsets and submissive photography. I like to shoot in natural light and in different locations... the edgier the better! For me, transferring the image from my mind to the photograph is, and still remains, a thrill...

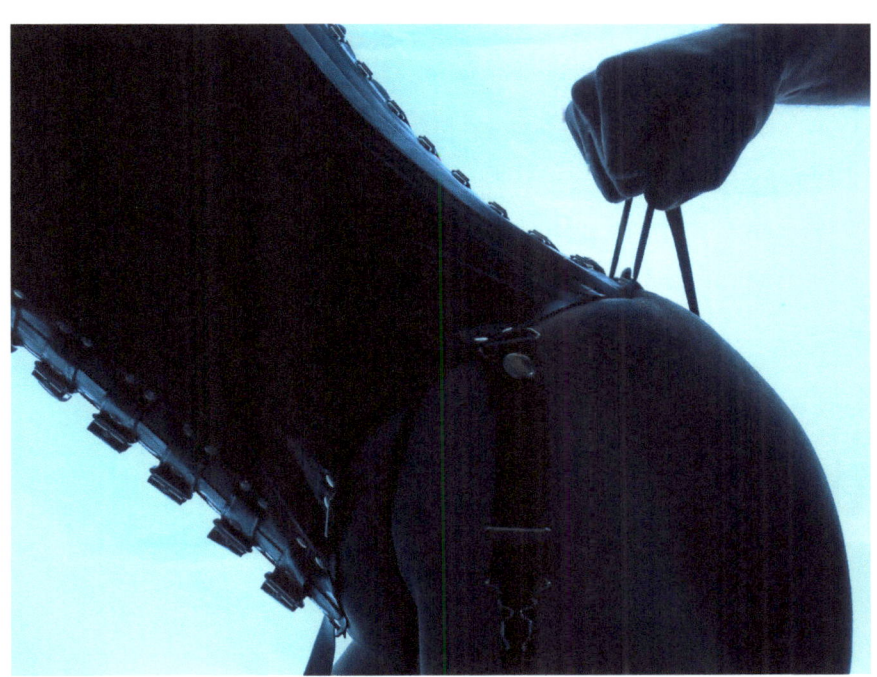

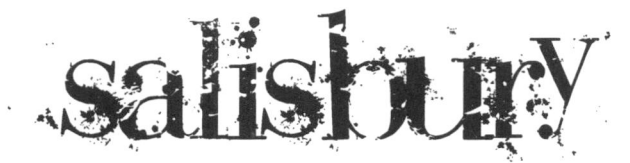

salisbury

Henny Penny's Expose (she's an easy lay)

*Fragile, fertile, raw and such a simple form. Medium and pigment
are subtly glazed to create the shadowed world of the
cradled egg - Shhhh!*

Laura Salisbury

*Laura Salisbury paints primarily in acrylic. Her painting
foundation in watercolor continues to influence her style
today. Recent works show a minimalist approach to render-
ing the subject in both color and medium through glazing.
Laura received art education at the University of Saskatch-
ewan, and has participated in various programs at OUC and
KAG. Laura's work has been shown at Innovation Place
UofS,at Rotary Center for the Arts, at Kelowna Art
Gallery,and can be seen at Gallery 421.*

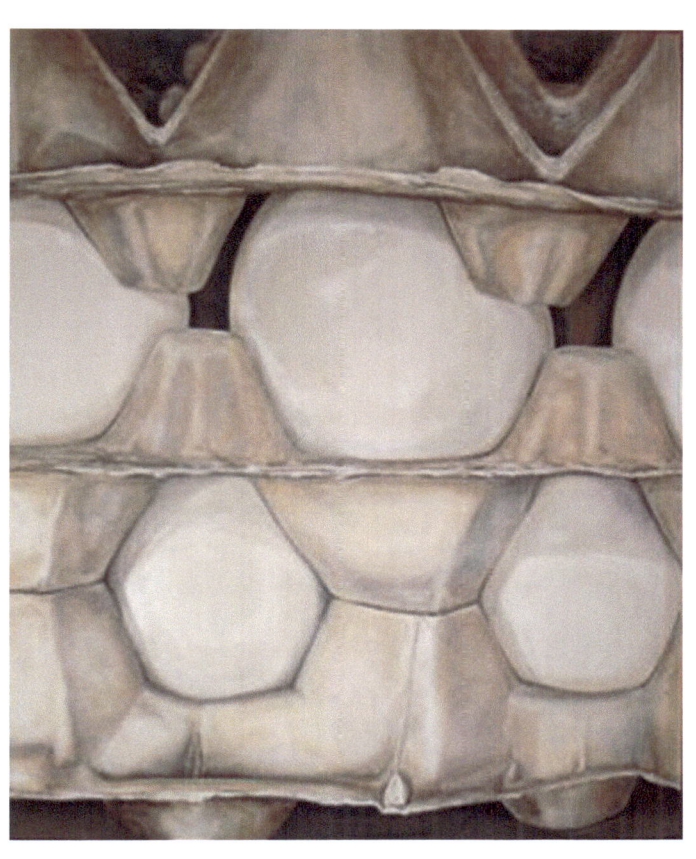

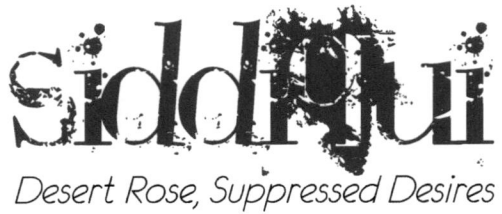

Desert Rose, Suppressed Desires

If only the walls could speak in the oil rich desert kingdoms, her needs, wants and desires might be heard.

Tina Siddiqui

Over 25 years of experience as an exhibiting artist and an art instructor. Awarded for protraiture, abstract painting and art education. Painting in a variety of mediums I have particapted in shows in Canada, United Kingdom, Pakistan and United Arab Emirates. Born and raised in Pakistan, educated as a Graphic Designer and lived in various locations in the Middle East from an early age. Kelowna became home in 2004 after a stay of 13 years in Dubai. Am I in Heaven or what?

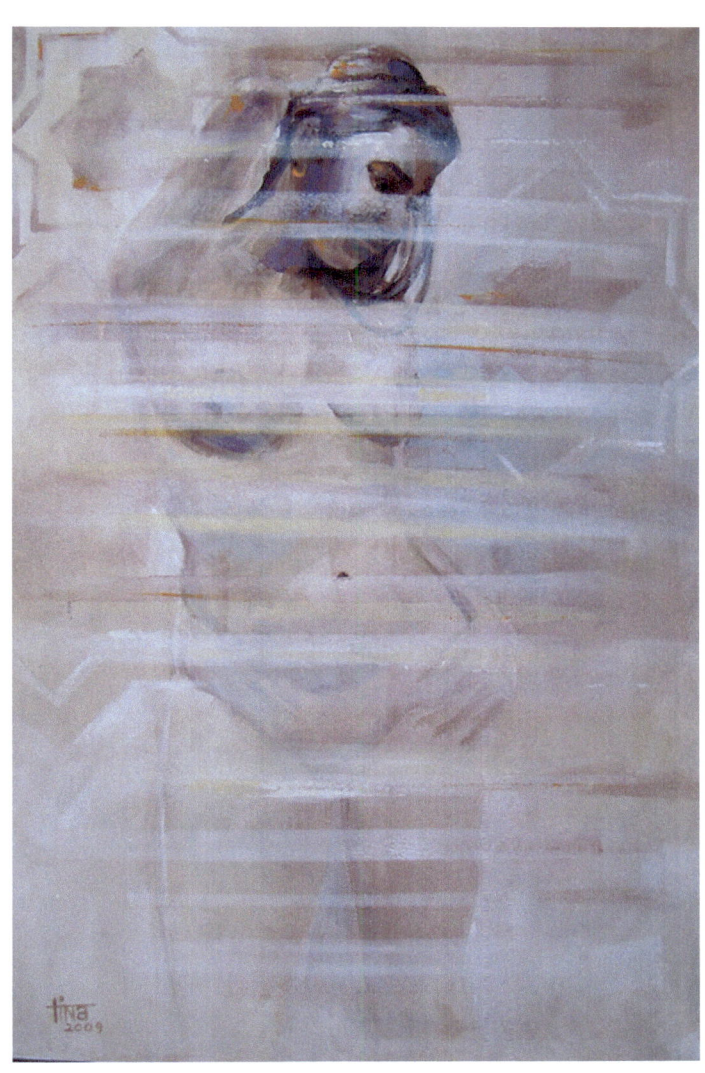

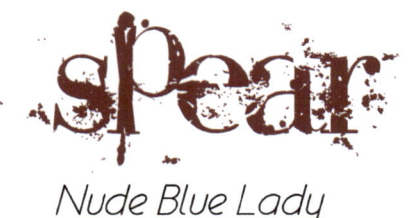

Nude Blue Lady

this painting is the inspiration and interpretation
of the athletic side of ourselves

Carrol Spear

Carrol Spear is a self taught local artist working from her at
home gallery in the Westside of Kelowna, B.C. With her
brushes flying, her passion and flair for art are demonstrated
in a variety of artistic styles.

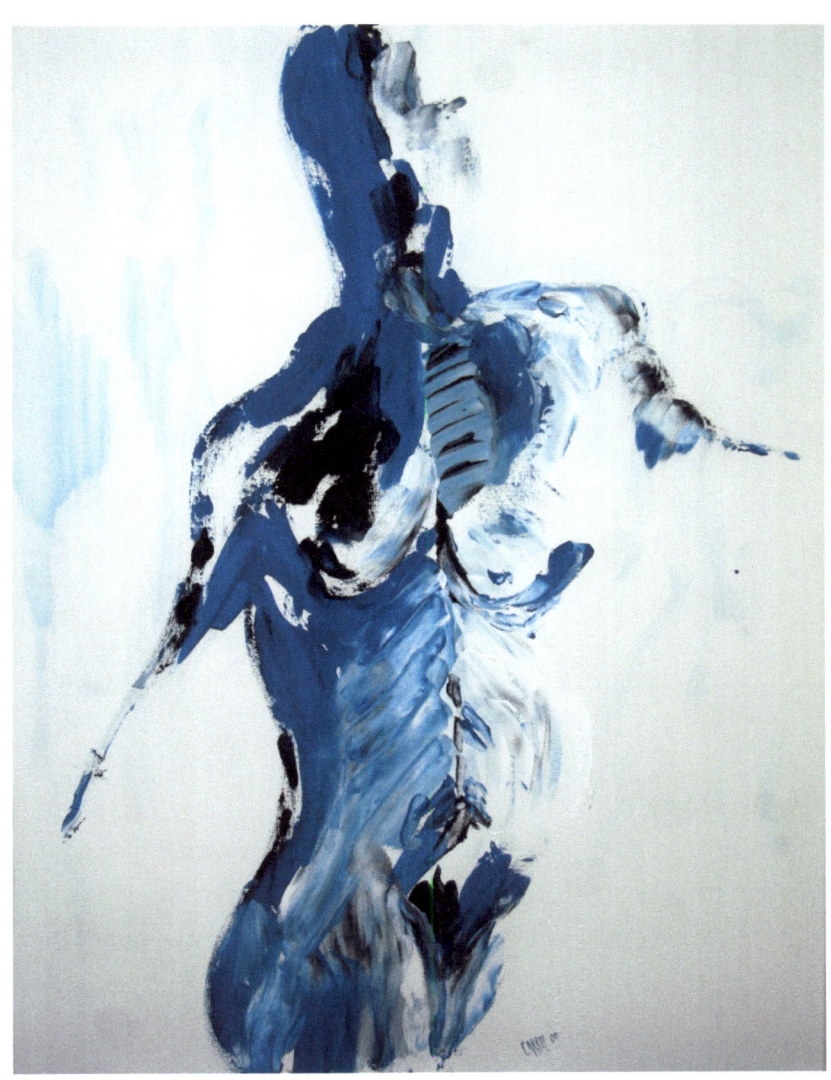

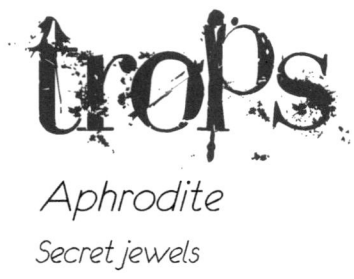

Aphrodite

Secret jewels

Julia Trops

Julia left Calgary at the age of 22 to join the military., and spent 12 years in the Canadian Air Force and living across Canada, including serving a peacekeeping mission in the Middle East, in the Sinai Desert. After retirement in 1997, she received a Bachelor of Fine Arts with Great Distinction in 2001 from the University of Lethbridge with a focus on Studio Arts. In 2002, in competition with 78 other candidates, Julia was chosen to be one of 6 resident artists in the new Rotary Centre for the Arts. Julia has been published as a writer and an artist in various magazines and books. Julia's work is represented by three galleries and she is a very active member in the Kelowna arts and cultural community.

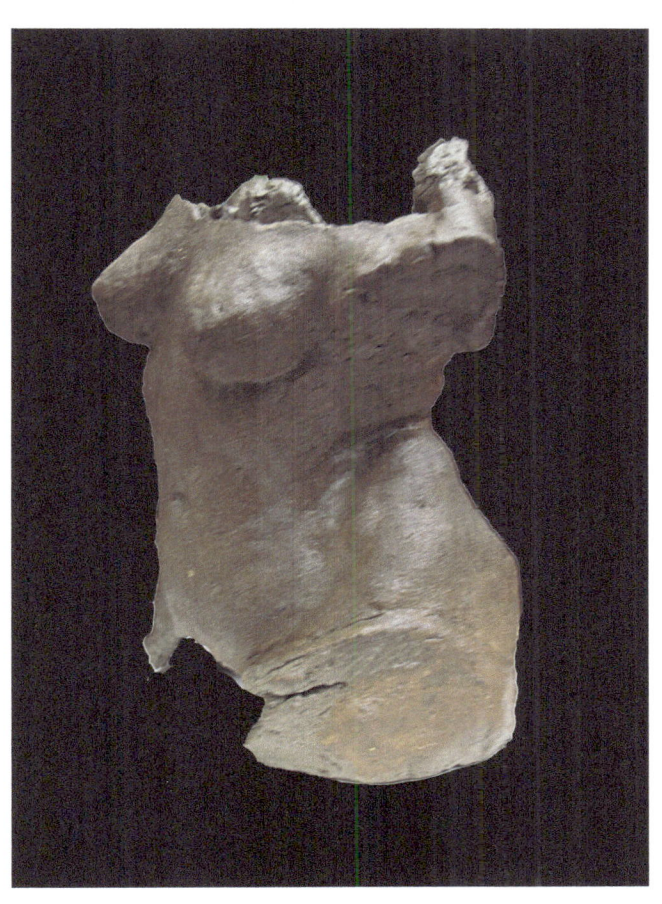

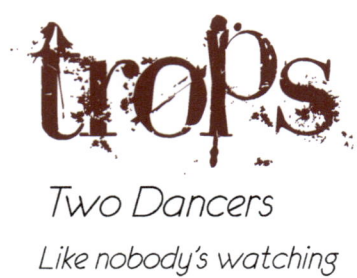

Two Dancers

Like nobody's watching

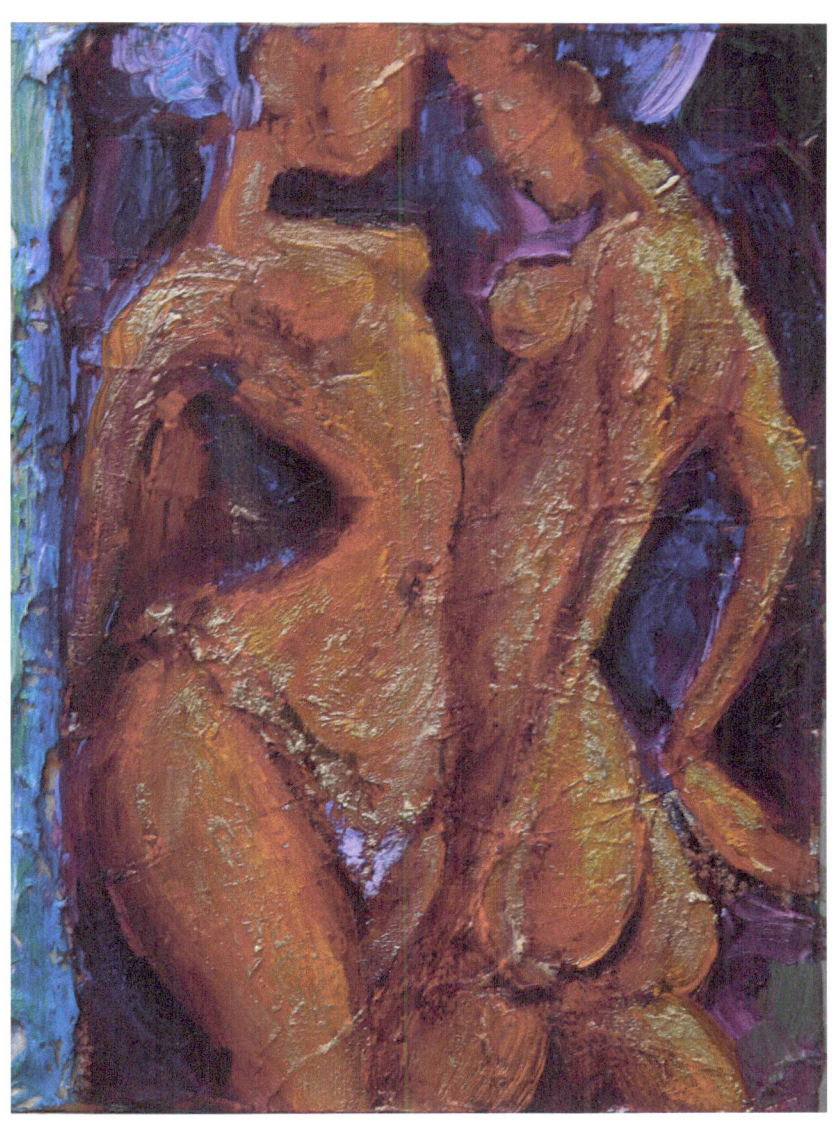

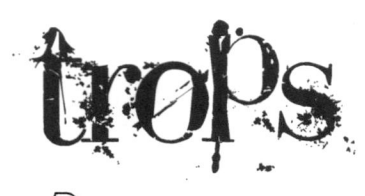

Danae

Time well spent

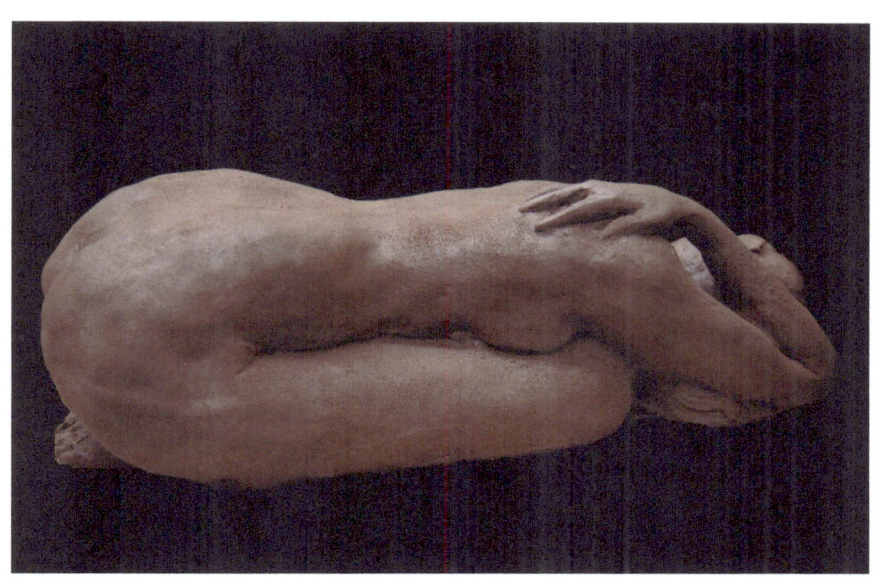

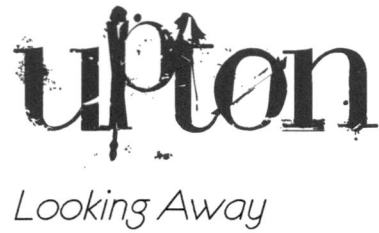

Looking Away

Katherine Upton

B Ed UBC double fine arts major. Painting and art criticism Art Students League of New YorkKatherine taught art in BC secondary schools for twenty years. For ten years she and her family sailed their yacht in the South Pacific. Katherine sketched and painted while cruising, and held solo exhibitions in Brisbane, Australia and in Lae, Papua New Guinea. After retirement in 2003, the Uptons moved to Vernon, into a house overlooking Swan Lake. An early project converted the double garage into a studio. It is in this wonderfully transformed space that Katherine now works.

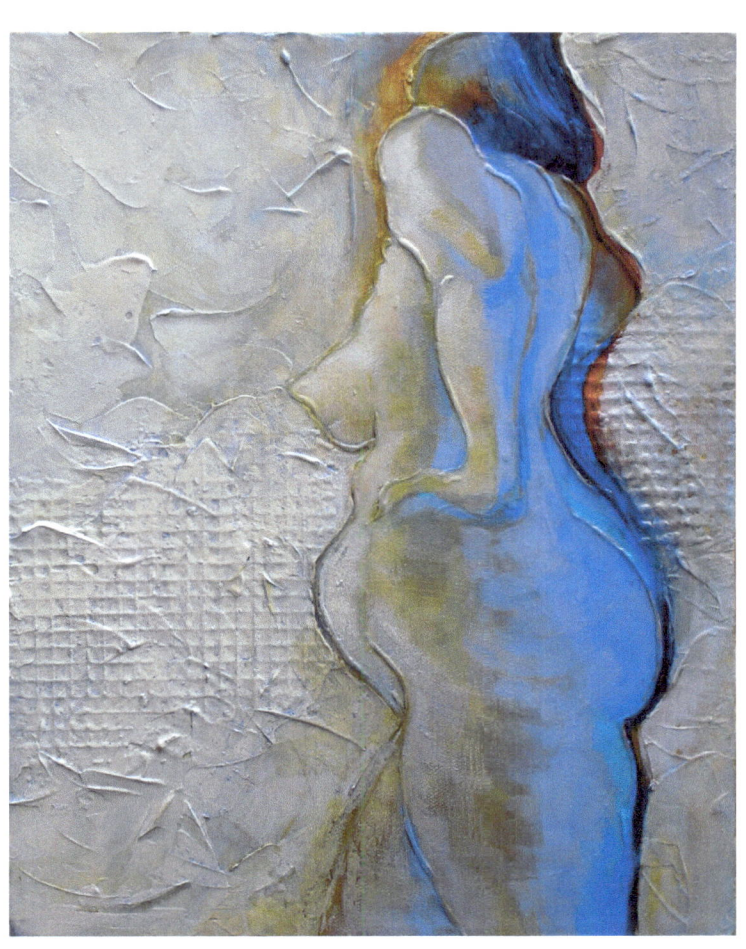

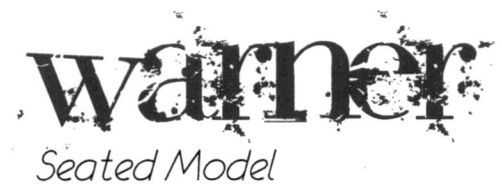

warner

Seated Model

*There was something about this model that inspired
some of my better efforts. Wish I hadn't lost track of her!*

Craig Warner

*Craig Warner was born in Freeport, NY in 1950. A graduate
of the Nova Scotia College of Art and Design, he worked in
NYC as a graphic designer from 1979 to 2003. In 2003 he
relocated with his wife to her hometown of Vernon, BC. He is
an avid golfer and photographer, and a regular at the life
drawing open studio in Vernon.*

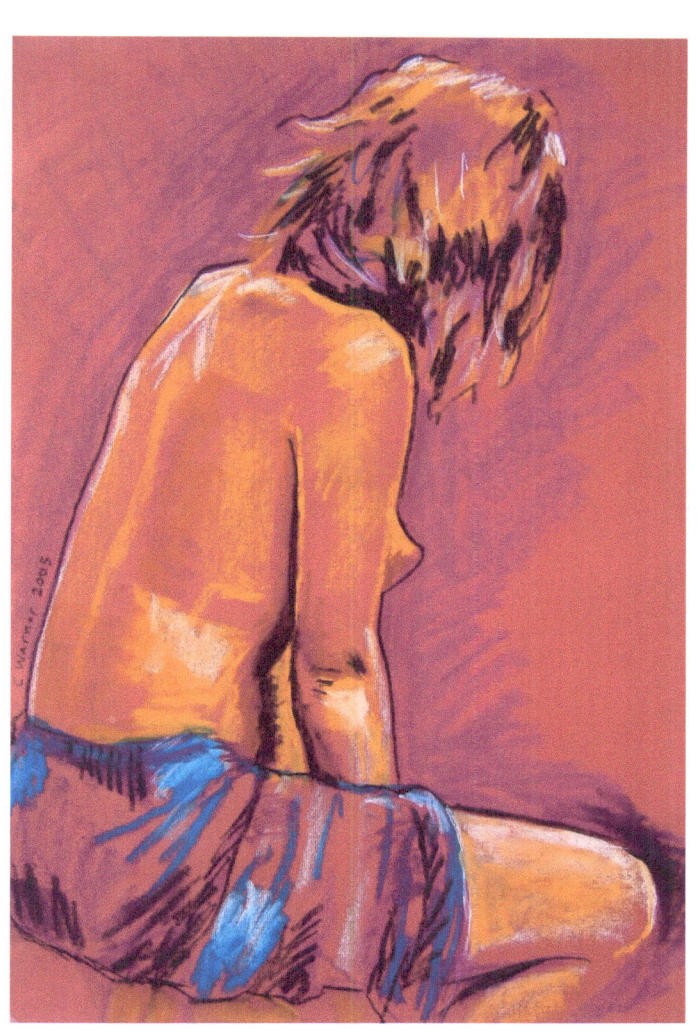

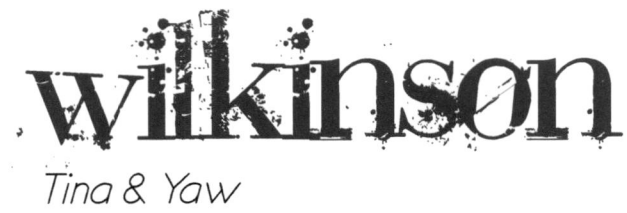

Tina & Yaw

The serenity of being held just tight enough

Diana Wilkinson

Diana Wilkinson is a self taught multimedia artist/photographer who's passion has evolved with discreet, tasteful black and white nude photography. She believes there is beauty and grace in all human shapes and seems to capture it by seeing beyond the layers of skin. Her ability to build a comfortable and trusting relationship during a photo shoot makes the experience powerful and enlightening for those involved. By contrast, her artwork (paper and pastel on canvas)is vividly colorful and tempts one to touch and feel.

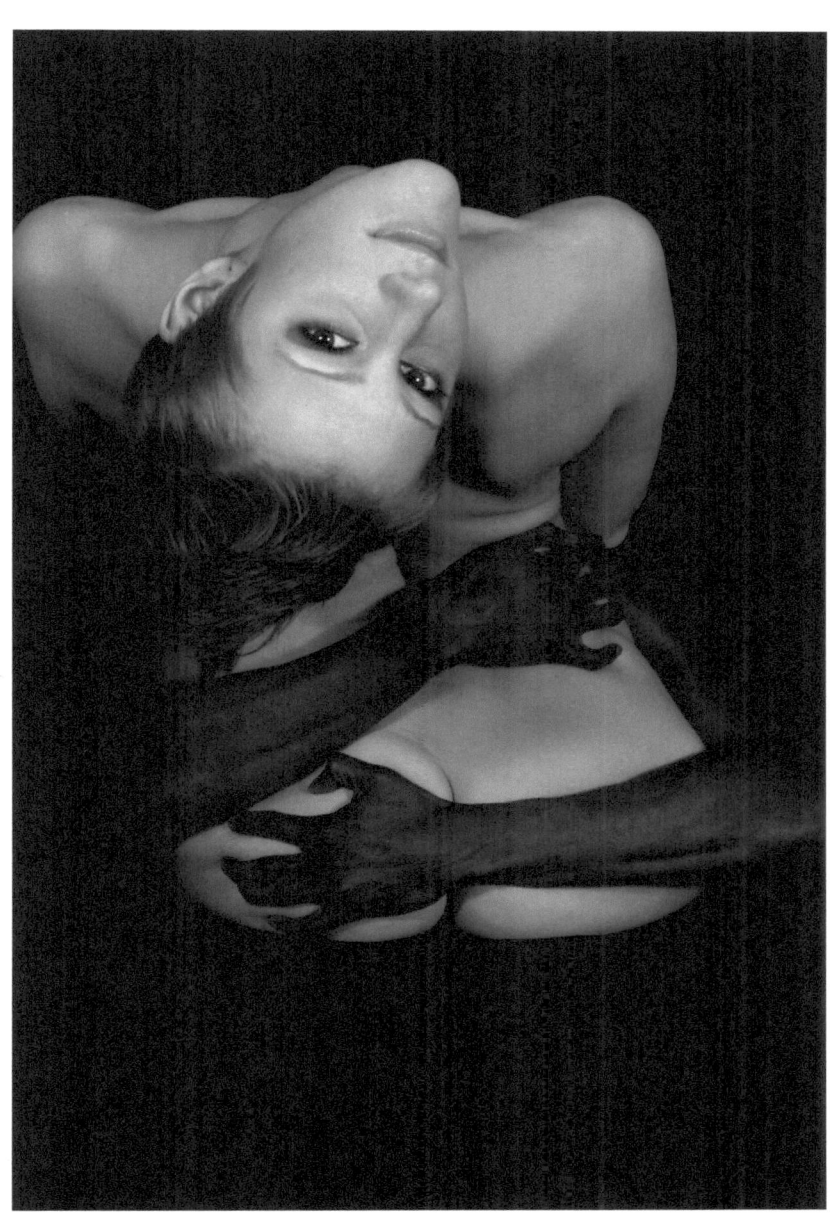

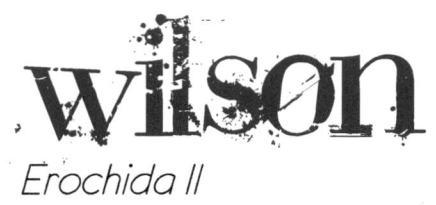

Erochida II

An abstract study of naturally intimate, and seductive forms that ultimately bring us closer to our selves.

Lauren Wilson

Practicing as a Self Representing Independant Artist, I am able to move quite freely between expressing myself via photography, drawing, painting, or textiles. I have an education background in textile art and design, I consider myself a figurative artist and one of my greatest joys is drawing from a live model, but I am also quite at home behind the lens of my camera! An everyday walk along the road, for me, can turn into a visual feast when reframed through the viewfinder. For some artists it may be important to develop a particular style that makes them identifi-able, for me it is important that regardless of style, the work I produce is of the best quality and my passion for it shows.

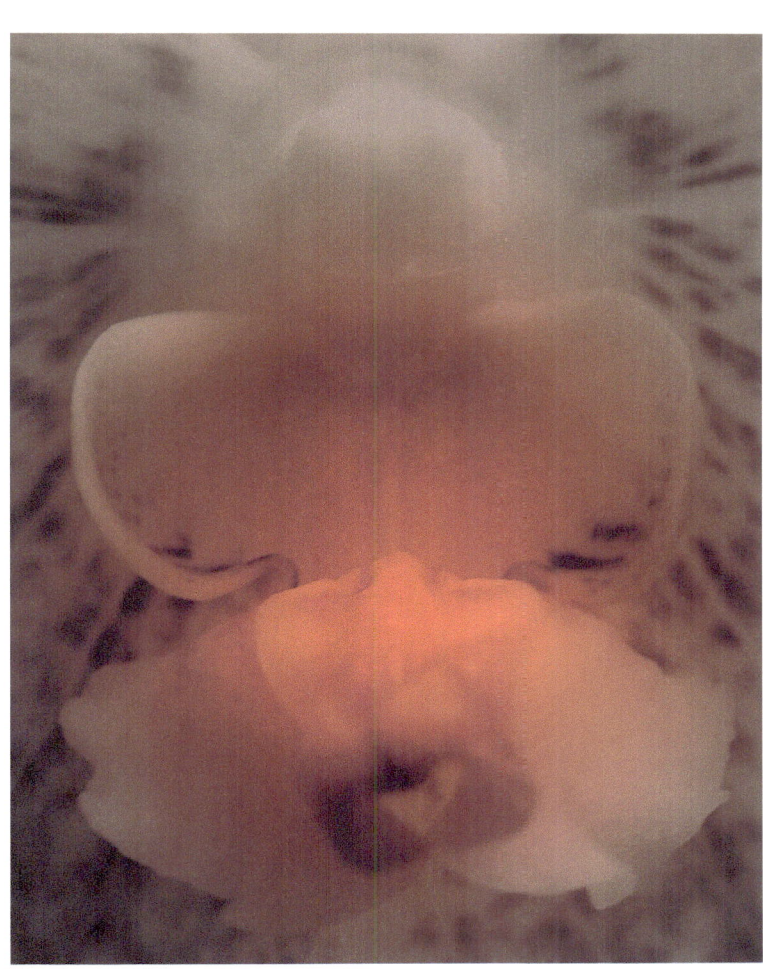

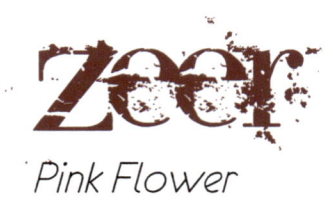

Pink Flower

As delicate, beautiful and bold as the flower in her hair.

Rob Zeer

Currently resides in Kelowna. Born 1956 in Weyburn Saskatch-ewan. He is mostly self taught but also received minor art study at the University Of Calgary and the Alberta College Of Fine Art. His main focus has been landscapes on canvas but he also draws and paints figures. Zeer currently exhibits and sells his work at Roberts Gallery in Toronto, Webster Galleries in Calgary and the Hambleton Gallery in Kelowna. His work with an editorial was recently featured in the 2009 winter edition of Magazine Art.

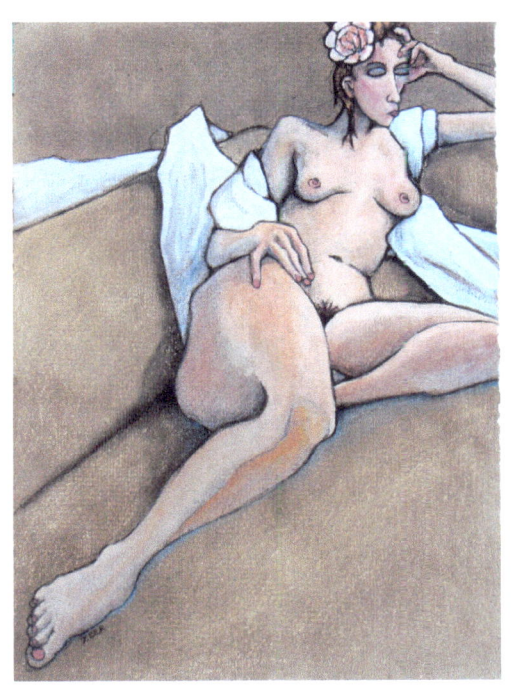

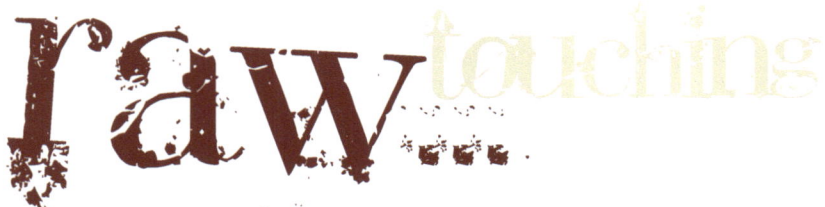

Iris Morden irismorden@telus.net   www.kelownasculptors.com
Ralph Critchlow rcritch@telus.net
Angela Hansen amhansen@telus.net   www.angelahansenart.com
Darryl W Funk d.atomikfunk@gmail.com   www.atomikfunk.com
Emmy Bouma boumaeb@shaw.ca
Cherie Hanson creative@hansonward.com   www.cheriehanson.com
Jennifer Burrows jennross@shaw.ca
                       www.fineartamerica.com/profiles/jennifer-burrows.html
Mel Hunt melvynhunt@hotmail.com   www.kelownasculptors.com
Bonnie Anderson pottersaddict@shawbiz.ca   www.bonnieandersonartist.com
Lynden Beesley lynbee@shaw.ca   www.atelierpom.com
Katherine Upton k.upton@shaw.ca   www.okanaganartistsleague.ca/upton.html
Tina Siddiqui taessuxmal@yahoo.com
Julia Trops juliatrops@gmail.com   www.juliatrops.com
Michele Nobel m.nobel@gmail.com
Yvonne Morrish ymorrish@shaw.ca   www.yvonnemorrish.ca
Carrie Harper thepear@telus.net   www.thepearworkshop.com
Laura Salisbury laga@shaw.ca   www.gallery421.ca/gallery/album36
Carol Hermesh art@carolhermesh.com   www.carolhermesh.com
Gabriel Dinim gdinim@netidea.com   www.lightmountainphotography.com
Diana Wilkinson dinyw3@hotmail.com   www.rynikaarts.com
TJ Critchlow tracijo@telus.net
Karen Close keclose@yahoo.com
Diana Creasey-Funk dcfunk@shaw.ca
Angella Goodon angellagoodon@shaw.ca   www.angellagoodon.com
Daniel McKellar dmck007@shaw.ca
Kevin Ade
Joyce Dalton shibley2001@yahoo.com
Carrol Spear cspear@shaw.ca   www.carrolskelownaartcreations.com
Craig Warner chwarner@shaw.ca
Aunaray C Clusiau soulfairy@shaw.ca
Rob Zeer robzeer@gmail.com
www.hambletongalleries.com/dynamic/artists/Rob_Zeer.asp
Lauren B Wilson laurenbwilson@hotmail.com   be2belauren.blogspot.com

www.ingramcontent.com/pod-product-compliance
Lightning Source LLC
Chambersburg PA
CBHW040826180526
45159CB00001B/80